Hogan Interior.

PATTERNS
AND
CEREMONIALS
OF THE INDIANS OF THE
SOUTHWEST

ILLUSTRATED BY

Ira Moskowitz

TEXT BY

John Collier

WITH AN INTRODUCTION BY

JOHN SLOAN

DOVER PUBLICATIONS, INC.
New York

Published in Canada by General Publishing Company, Ltd., 30 Lesmill Road, Don Mills, Toronto, Ontario.

Published in the United Kingdom by Constable and Company, Ltd., 3 The Lanchesters, 162–164 Fulham Palace Road, London W6 9ER.

Bibliographical Note

This Dover edition, first published in 1995, is an unabridged and unaltered republication of the work originally published by E. P. Dutton & Co., Inc., New York, in 1949, in an edition limited to 1,475 numbered and signed copies.

Library of Congress Cataloging-in-Publication Data

Collier, John, 1884–1968.
      Patterns and ceremonials of the Indians of the Southwest / illustrated by Ira Moskowitz ; text by John Collier ; with an introduction by John Sloan.
            p.   cm.
      Originally published: New York : Dutton, 1949.
      ISBN 0-486-28692-4 (pbk.)
      1. Indians of North America—Southwest, New—Rites and ceremonies.
2. Indian dance—Southwest, New.   I. Moskowitz, Ira.   II. Title.
E78.S7C6   1995
299′.74′0979—dc20   95-6513
                                                                              CIP

Manufactured in the United States of America
Dover Publications, Inc., 31 East 2nd Street, Mineola, N.Y. 11501

INTRODUCTION
by John Sloan

THE *publication of this handsome book about the Indians of our South-west affords me a pleasant opportunity to say a few words of introduction about the rich collection of pictures with which it is illustrated.*

The first time I saw the Santo Domingo Corn Dance I felt the same strong emotion from the rhythm of the drums and primitive intensity of that age-old dance ritual that I experienced when I saw Isadora Duncan fill the stage of the Metropolitan Opera House with her great personality. It is not necessary to understand an art (in fact, I don't think that even the creator understands his work) in order to react to it. And for too long the American Indians have been considered an anomaly in the modern world because they live the simple life of artists. It is only recently that their handicrafts and dance ceremonies have been recognized as art rather than ethnological curiosities.

The pictorial approach of the European to the representation of the life and customs of our American Indians has taken many and diverse points of view. A factual, documentary or sentimental attitude has been taken by most of the illustrators, photographers and artists who have approached this subject matter.

Early publications illustrating the accounts of explorers and travelers are often embellished with figments of the graphic imagination which, in the light of our acquired knowledge of the Indian customs and costumes, are palpably erroneous or absurd. Old drawings and prints depicting pseudo-classical athletes and vestal virgins and bacchantes may be amusing and quaint, but their value as art or portrayal of Indian life is very slight. Even when the artist or illustrator has had contact on the spot, his records show a lack of sympathy or understanding of the Indian as a fellow human.

Later, in the years during and following our successful conquest and

5

Introduction

attempts to exterminate the early American, he has been represented as a savage bent on murder, fire and pillage, practicing treachery so quickly learned from his European guests.

During the last century serious artists have left us portrayals of Indian chiefs and factual drawings showing modes of life which are of some historical importance. Also of great value to the student and collector are the drawings and photographs made by and for the ethnologists.

The graphic work of the Indians themselves has been largely confined to a kind of pictograph style, records of this kind being painted on skins and incised on stone. About thirty-five years ago, Dr. Edgar L. Hewett started to encourage the Southwestern Indians to make drawings of their ceremonial dances in water color. For a time, especially before we began to influence them by instruction and tourist patronage, they produced finely stylized drawings which add to their distinction as artists and to our knowledge of their costumes and rituals.

In contrast with all this rather documentary representation, the drawings and lithographs by Ira Moskowitz are notable for an emotional response to the Indian life. He may be called a representational or realistic draftsman, terms now in disrepute among the moderns, but in my estimation this quality places his work in line with the great tradition of the past which produced giants like Rembrandt and Daumier. The ultramodern movement has been a great medicine for adult artists, pointing the way back to technical understanding of the mature work of the past and the products of primitive cultures. Too many of our younger followers of the modern school, however, are just doodling. They lack humility in the face of nature.

I like Ira Moskowitz's work because he approaches the Indian not with curiosity, but with friendliness, respect and awe. He records the feelings of a sympathetic fellow human in the presence of a culture ages older than our own.

We have many races and religious sects in this country, but the living culture of the Southwestern Indians stands high in significance among them. Crowned by the ages of time, the traditions of their ancestors have been

Introduction

preserved and revitalized through their art and religious ceremonials. Ira Moskowitz has felt this primitive religious life, but he has not taken the liberty of attempting to portray the ceremonies in panorama. Rather he has selected incidents which impressed him personally.

These pictures are not intended to be mere records of the costumes and habitat of the Indian, although quite true in observation and suggestion. No artist is in competition with the camera as an instrument for documentation. Ira Moskowitz lived with the Indians, he enjoyed their humor, understood their simple way of life and appreciated their deep religious feeling. His drawings are works of art, being the honest reaction of an artist to life. For this reason they do more than embellish the pages of this book: decorative illustrations or photographs might suffice for that. The work of a real artist, in a technique familiar to our European-trained minds, should do much to awaken our understanding of the Indian people, whose attitude toward art is so much nobler, traditionally, than ours.

The Indian lives with art as a commonplace and a necessity. His useful things are made with an eye for permanent beauty, the acts of his daily life are performed with a sense of timelessness, his religious feeling and tradition are based on contact with reality. As John Collier points out in his wise and warmly written text, the life of the Indians should serve as an example and a warning to our hurried materialist civilization.

TO MY TEACHER HARRY WICKEY
AND TO MY FRIEND MRS. HOWARD E. WURLITZER

IRA MOSKOWITZ.

CONTENTS

ILLUSTRATIONS

Section 1. TAOS

Illustrations

Illustrations

Section 4. APACHE, MESCALERO AND JICARILLA

Section 5. HOPI

Section 6. NAVAJO, Part I

Illustrations

*The Lithographs from which these reproductions were made
were printed for the Artist by Mr. Hill Sharp, of
Muncie, Indiana.*

Chapter 1

ANOTHER TIME DIMENSION
THAN OURS

THESE Southwestern Indians have much that we know we need. And they have one possession, the most distinguishing of all, which we have forgotten that we need. Rather, perhaps, we dare not hope to make it our own.

That possession is *a time sense* different from ours, and happier. Once our white race had it too, and then the mechanized world took it away from us. Each of us has experienced that other and happier time sense in young childhood, and then we moved into the lockstep of clockwork time. We think, now, that any other time than linear, chronological time is an escapist dream. The Indians tell us otherwise, and their message and demonstration addresses itself to one of our deepest distresses and most forlorn yearnings.

We bow to clockwork time. We think we must yield to it our all—body, conduct and soul. Strange vortex in the ocean of life, created by intellect and by the machine only yesterday in our racial history, and in hard contradiction with vital and spiritual instinct: such is clockwork time, necessary as a tool, deadly as a master.

But we think it is our master, and here the Indians will gainsay us. And clockwork time—the event which in unmusical synchrony marches to the beat of the minutes, the hours, the onrushing and vanishing years of linear time—sweeps us and inwardly impels us faster and faster on. And enough of clockwork time we never have—never. And we abide so briefly, within that rush of linear time which subconsciously we experience as a kind of panic rout; and we are old, so soon, and we are done, and we hardly had time to live at all.

Not that we choose that life shall be that way. Did there exist—as the Indians in their whole life affirm—a dimension of time—a reality of time—not linear, not clock-measured, clock-controlled, and clock-ended for us, we would be glad; we would enter it, and expand our being there. There are

15

human groups, normal, and efficient in difficult ways of the world, which do thus expand their being, and the tribal Indians are among them.

In solitary, mystical experience many of ourselves do enter another time dimension. But under the frown of clockwork time which claims the world, we place our experience out in an eternity beyond the years and beyond the stars. Not out there did the other time dimension originate, in racial history, but within the germ plasm and the organic rhythms and the social soul; nor is its reference only or mainly to the moveless eternity. It is life's instinct and environment, and human society's instinct and environment. To realize it or not realize it makes an enormous difference, even a decisive difference. The Indians realize it, and they can make us know.

There comes from England, by boat mail, a manuscript chapter of a book not yet published. Its writer is a British colonial administrator, recently lecturer on colonial administration at Oxford University, now returned to colonial service in Melanesia. Adrian Dobbs is his name; a man of experience wide and profound. And his subject proves to be *the time dimension,* examined as a practical factor in the administration or servicing of the billion of "pre-industrial" inhabitants of Asia and Africa.

Time, Adrian Dobbs suggests, does veritably have, for organisms, souls and societies, a dimension different from, and in contrast with, that merely linear dimension which our machines, clocks and calendars insist on. One, two, three, and thus on without pause or end, goes linear time; the synchronized future is hurtled remorselessly across the knife-edge present into a time-ordered past where nothing changes, moves or acts forever. But not thus, Adrian Dobbs insists, does time appear to the Buddhists of Ceylon, to the Gaels of the wild northwest coast of Ireland, and to many another branch of the human race.

In the mind of Buddhist Ceylon, in its private and public behavior, in its work rhythms and play rhythms, its private and public expectancies, linear time is not the only and not the controlling time. Instead, time as experienced and lived by Buddhist Ceylon is no linear instant wherein all real events march lockstep from nought to nought; time is enduring and commanding future, which hurtles not across the narrow present to become immured in a linear past—enduring future which draws the present on and on. And time is enduring past, which is not dead and gone, which can enter and does enter the knife-edge present, but whose fundamental relationship is with the enduring future. In human reality, in Ceylon, this *other* time dimension contains the linear dimension as a sometimes phantasmal, sometimes insubordinate and unreconciled, lesser part; in the final event, it is lord over linear time.

Hence, human experience in Ceylon has an atmosphere and meaning and value somewhat different from experience with you and me. Life has an inner spaciousness greater than yours or mine. The capacity to wait, to endure, to possess the things that seem gone, and to strive, and socially to create, is somewhat different from ours. Dobbs believes that the difference is momentous, practically as well as emotionally and spiritually, and he asks: What will result, in changed world events, if the clock-mindedness of the modern, industrial West shall equate itself with the enduring-past and enduring-future mindedness of peoples like the Ceylonese? And how far representative, in this matter, are the Ceylonese?

My mind goes to a certain American Indian tribe, one of those which are pictured in this book. The Tewan pueblo, Tesuque, is practically within the suburbs of Santa Fe, in New Mexico. Its contact with the white world has been a thing of every day, now into its fifth post-Columbian century. Tesuque is a tiny city-state; its population is one hundred and fifty souls. Tesuque is at home in the white world. Economically and politically, it is a cooperative commonwealth, efficient, sophisticated, and of undeviating public virtue; but the virtue contains within itself no puritan gloom. Tesuque functions, when need be, and through a secondary adaptation, along the narrow edge of linear Western time.

In the autumn of 1922, I had occasion for long and absorbed meetings with the Governor of Tesuque and his Council of Principal Men. Whites had seized nearly all of Tesuque's irrigable land. Legislation had been forced through the Senate by the Interior Department at Washington, designed to legalize the whites' seizure of the tribe's lands. The bill momentarily might pass in the House, and was assured of Presidential signature. And a drive to exterminate the Pueblos' ancient religions had been launched by the government. Tesuque at that date was subsisting (I did not then know the fact, because the Tesuques never mentioned their bodily hunger) on a per capita income of a few cents over sixteen dollars a year, including all produce grown and consumed.

Gradually, as our meetings progressed, and as Martin Vigil of Tesuque enlightened me by interpretation, I came to realize that I had entered a time dimension not like that of the white world from which I had come. These men and women were living in a time a thousand years ago. An event of many thousand years of group volition, no part of it lapsed into a dead past, was travailing across the present into a future of unknown thousands of years. Toward that "enduring future," the tribe's being and soul was winging like a migrating bird along its ancient migration route. So intense was the reality of this effort of flight between the "twin eternities" of past and future, that all minor aspects fell into oblivion. Personal contingency, personal fate simply did not figure at all. Hunger did not figure. A white well-wisher in Santa Fe discovered that the little tribe was in famine, and set in motion a newspaper campaign for relief. The Tesuques smiled, because the diversion from their real issue was friendly meant; they stayed with their real issue.

A violent action was in process (this was how the Tesuques viewed their crisis), an action directed from the outside against the tribe. The action was designed to kill what the white man called the Indians' past, by shattering the bridge of tribal land and tribal religion which united past and future—the bridge on which the deathless two-way journey plied from living past to living future, living future to living past. Meeting the crisis, the "twin eternities" merged their brooding power; and this they did at each of the twenty-one menaced pueblos in New Mexico, of which Tesuque was one. The result was planned action in the linear present—action which will be mentioned at its place in this book; the action marked and made the beginning of the historic change in governmental policy which revolutionized the situation of all Indians. But at this point, the subject is the time dimension of tribal Indian life, that all-conserving abysm of time wherein is no past wholly gone and no future wholly inert.

On another occasion, some years later, at a pueblo which I may not name, the tribe's priestly representative was assisting for initiation into the tribe a young man from another pueblo who had married a girl of this pueblo. Much that he told this young man, the teacher was not free to tell to me. But part of the tutelage was the unveiling of the hidden names and the spiritual meanings of hundreds of physical places, wide over the land. Mesas, plinths, streams and springs; forests that existed no more, trails unused for hundreds of years. Some of the places had vanished utterly with the passage of linear time; the highest mountain peak, in one of the sacred areas along the Rocky Mountain range, was the highest no longer, and the tree line had moved downward two hundred vertical feet since these tribal

Another Time Dimension Than Ours

memories, as we would call them, this tribal present, as the Indians knew it, had been born. The memories, the present, spanned geological time.

"But, Geronimo," I remarked, "your tribe does not own these places and boundaries any more." He replied: "We own them in our soul."

In those years, I still took for granted our modern fatalism: that the Indian's spirit, and all aboriginal and ancient spirit, had to die. Omnipotent clockwork time must engulf all. The glory and power of that other time dimension would have to yield to the cosmopolitan century. I knew it would mean diminishing the human stature, draining the dearest meaning out of the universe, the stripping away of his uniquely vital and human part from man, the greater dominance of mechanism over life. But it had to be, I believed; and only in solitary, mystical experience, thereafter, would all-conserving and prophetic, dynamic, creative time be known.

The ensuing twenty-five years seem to have proved that the fatalism was wrong, not only as applied to the American tribal Indian but as applied to groups in many parts of the world. That time dimension not linear, which was of ancient man, bestows a power to endure, to create, and to outlast; a motive and a power to bend means to ends; it has a survival value biological and social; it is central to man, and this age of commanding externalism, which seems to have engulfed so much of our white life, may yet fail to engulf the human time dimension.

In the Americas at least, Indian societies which live by the time dimension not only linear, the conserving and future-containing dimension, are re-asserting themselves in all the lands from the Arctic shores to southern Chile. And in the American Southwest, recent years have witnessed a deeply exciting event. Ancient tribes, in order that their living past shall not die, and under the impulsion of their living future, have utilized the modern technologies and organizational forms with brilliant effectiveness; they have triumphed along the roaring assembly line of linear time, in ways which the clock-conditioned observer finds to be practical and momentous. That other time dimension, which Adrian Dobbs finds in Asia, is no mere subjectivism, no mere and sterile dream of the Ceylonese and the Hopi and Tewan and Keresan and Zuñian and California Wintun soul. It is a society-building, action-sustaining, wisdom-giving and health-giving and world-shaping endowment, which humanity will not permanently do without.

Chapter 2

THE LAND AND ITS
INDIAN PEOPLES

THE splendor of the universe of things"—such is the upland portion of the American Southwest.

A high land—from 5,000 to 13,000 feet high. A land of dry, translucent air, of stupendous cloud effects and sudden, brief lightning storms. Between great, far-separated mountains that rise alone, and wild wildernesses of mountains, as east and north from the Rio Grande pueblos, the vast plateau-plains roll on and on. Mountainous sand dunes, white as snow; painted desert, blood-red and of all rainbow hues; high forests of the witchlike aspen, and great forests of nondeciduous trees; man-ruined land, thousands upon thousands of square miles of wind-eroded and water-eroded range, the wreckage of a mere sixty to seventy years. Whole watersheds man-wounded all almost mortally, whose herdsmen and irrigationists, lonely hogan homes, and villages and cities, are doomed unless the earth wounds can be healed.

And ice caves and bat caves; immense black lava flows; canyons geologically eroded, whose sudden drop from the level plains is thousands of feet, and on whose walls the earth record of a billion years can be read; the Grand Canyon, which bounds this wizard land to the west, is only one of these canyons.

And ruins—thousands of ruins. Cliff dwellings and cities of cliff dwellings, and dead pueblos sinking into dust by stream side or out on the wide plain.

And rolling through and across it all, rolling through and across even the man-ruined lands, such splendor and power of sun, of blazing and glooming clouds, of rains blown in long gray veils from clouds seen afar, to return to cloud without ever moistening the plain; and such brilliance of stars in the desert night, as dwellers in Eastern America and Europe hardly can imagine. Nature strikes a chord out there which wildly exhilarates the soul, a cosmical chord, and it is one chord through all that myriadly contrasting land.

The Land and Its Indian Peoples

Such is the Pueblos', the Navajos', the Apaches' land. It has been their land, and they its human embodiment, for so many thousand years that no one knows the number. And here is one of the reasons why white men find these Indians so magnetic, so exciting, so healing and regenerating to starved human natures: that these Indians live their lives within the rhythms of this cosmical land. Far back within the Stone Age, they knew themselves as children of this land, and as co-workers with it in the universal process. They wrought this land into their world myths, their religions, their verbal poetry, and song and dance and ritual drama, even into their manual crafts and their costumes. They believed they were old as the land was old, eternal as it was eternal. Their soul, they believed, was its soul. And the marvelous symbol systems which they wrought out long ago in the Stone Age—symbol systems which had the cosmical union of man and earth as their central theme, and which structured the tribal world views and the societies and even the individual personalities: these symbol systems, and all the freight they bore, have moved across the centuries of white contact, and are the living power of these Indians now. White men come a little bit within that sway, and first they know a disturbing yet thrilling strangeness, and then they know: this is my native land; home of my own soul, as my own race possessed it long ago, and then possessed it no more. This is my recovered eternity!

Such exaltation the white friend feels, when he enters a little way into these tribes' lives. But always an anxious sadness succeeds the exaltation. *Can they go on in their joy and wonder where the marvel of earth transmutes itself into the marvel of souls?*

Can they go on (not only their flesh and blood, but their institutional and spiritual genius) in this modern, this American melting-pot world?

The first-impression reply would be: Almost certainly they can not go on.

That was my own belief, at the end of my first year amongst them, twenty-five years ago.

Their answer (the Indians'), with solemn purpose and assurance in the case of the New Mexico and Arizona pueblos at least, is wholly the opposite: "We will to go on, and we shall go on."

They have lived the "dangerous" life, have breasted tides of change, in prehistory, and not only since the white man came; they have incorporated change following upon change; and their continuity has not been broken, the inward and outward direction of their group genius has not been altered.

Indians of the Southwest

They are not inchoate societies, but subtly structured ones, and not petrified societies, but constantly evolving, developing ones, now as of old. They hold their profundities, but they are thoroughly efficient and practical too. They do not fear the world.

In truth, no man can give the answer: that these Indians in their institutions and spirit shall or shall not go on. No man can even answer another question, now: Shall human society and the human spirit go on? This text will recite some evidence from old-time and recent Southwestern Indian experience, it will be on the hopeful side, for Indian continuance. But the final answer will be supplied by the communal will of the tribes themselves. There are words quoted by Poe in *Lygeia,* from an ancient source:

"Man does not yield himself to the angels, or to death utterly, save through the weakness of his own feeble will."

No feeble will is that of the tribes of the American Southwest.

Meantime, whatever the future holds, there in the Southwest bloom now those marvelous gardens of the soul. From the Dawn Man there plies onward a strange and beautiful effort of social creation. With intensity and complete faith, the affirmation is renewed from thousands of years ago: Man is a spirit, and man and the living Earth Mother are no strangers or foes, each to each; and spiritual energy and passion, within peace, are within the scope of men.

Chapter 3

THE MANY-SIDEDNESS AND SOPHISTICATION OF THE TRIBES

THERE is no single, exclusive way to view a race or a people. There is no single, exclusive way to view even one detached individual. "We get what we bring," said Emerson, and that is a truth although not the full truth. "We understand only that which we love," said Goethe, and that is nearer to being a full truth.

Is one's soul enhungered for storm? Storm, great darknesses, motions titanic he will find in the Southwestern highland, and he will find them in the Indians. Is one's soul enhungered for peace, and for tranquillity within intensity? He will find in that highland such peace as there is in the movement of the Milky Way from east to west in the desert night. He will find marmoreal peace in the gray canyons on the Rio Grande pueblo country, the peace of the mystic rose in all of the Navajo painted desert; and he will find peace in the Indian heart and in the slow, cyclic rhythms of the Indian ceremonial year. If one wants the past, it is waiting him in the Southwest; there, in the Indian life, the arc of the social past has a greater span than any to be found in Europe: the arc in terms of evolutionary social change, not merely of years. And if one wants the present, and effort and struggle and invention and discovery in the attempted solution of almost insoluble present problems, he will find it right there where the ancientness is most alive— among the Navajos and among the Arizona and New Mexico Pueblos.

And if one wants a microcosm of our whole human world in crisis, this too he will find in the Navajo and Hopi country and at Zuñi, Laguna, Acoma pueblos and along the Rio Grande; and if he wants emergent social-economic political forms which are predictive of a future world not totalitarian and not ravenous-capitalist, he need not go to Scandinavia or Palestine, Switzer-

Indians of the Southwest

land or New Zealand; he can go to the Mescalero and Jicarilla Apache reservations and to some other Indian areas of the Southwest.

Any human grouping existing through long time, and coping with its tumult of inward being and with the hard world, must develop into many-sidedness if it is to survive at all. It cannot be only practical, or only mystical, or only artistic, or only Dionysian, or only Apollonian, or only spiritual, or only technological. Without active many-sidedness the group will perish from the earth.

This statement applies with greatest force precisely to those ancient, small, face-to-face, "primary" social groupings which the Indian tribes of the Southwest represent. Right on into the present, across past aeons, these statistically small Indian societies have had to be effectual molders of the personalities of their members; have had to be politically competent, industrially competent; have had to draw out from their few numbers versatile and concentrated powers of judgment, enduring courage, action, and therefore have had to achieve a true, deep democracy and to sustain it. Their many-sidedness has been increased by their intense romanticism of religion, their belief that the universe is a living being and that the universe requires of man an inner concentration and a sustained action of desire and will, to the end that the universe itself may "carry on." This inner concentration and sustained volition or prayer is not, among the Southwestern Indians, typically a solitary contemplation, but is a ritualized, a group self-intensification, with rich material symbolism and with song, dance, and mass drama. And this most inward activity is, in their own belief, their most practically necessary and productive activity among all others. And in this belief they are factually correct, not the less so though their cosmical dream be but a dream; for these incomparable religious expressions are incomparable educational forces too; they form the Indian soul and being, perpetually renew it, induct each generation into the whole of the heritage, sustain the society, discipline as well as nurture its members, and insure their industry now, as in olden times they insured also their military efficiency. The tribal will to live is closely united with these communal religious inpourings and outpourings. But above all, at this point, the *balanced many-sidedness* of the Indian groups is stressed, and the crucial function of their cosmically oriented religions in producing the many-sidedness and holding it in poised union, each part with all the differing parts, in a community whose shared life is lived with confident power by all its members.

Many-sidedness and Sophistication of the Tribes

Many-sidedness, within a group whose genius is cooperative and democratic, means individual sophistication. The word is used in only one of its dictionary meanings: made wise through experience. Sophisticated, i.e., aware, discerning and detached, in relation to the self and the other. The word does not mean "possessed of much knowledge," but "possessed of understanding." I have not known anywhere, and do not hope to know, individuals more richly sophisticated than a great many whom I have known among Southwestern Indian tribes. Navajo medicine men and headmen, Apache council members, Pueblo principal men and governors and secret society leaders, Hopi village and ceremonial chiefs. Among such men, the rule of no decision short of unanimous decision proves practicable; and such men, given time and a minimum of unobtrusive technical counsel, can solve—they do repeatedly solve—problems of statesmanship involving radical readjustments within the Indian community.

Abroad in the world, people know the sophistication of the Southwestern tribes through knowing the products of their arts. Sophistication, old, deep, and yet ever young, is revealed in the pottery work, the painting, the basket work, the silverwork and weaving. Again, profound sophistication, as in the stately and gracious art, calm, but with passion—the passion of worlds and ages—moving through it, of the Shalako ceremony at Zuñi pueblo, the Red Deer Dance at Taos. But it is in the brooding meetings of tribal councils, in long conversations with old and young leaders of the tribes, and in the intimacy of the spacious home life of Pueblo and of Navajo hogan, that one experiences that sophistication of every day which makes him know: these people and their ways are not near their end, they are nothing frail. The sophistication of ancient China, of the Socratic circle or the Academe, of Father Zossima in *The Brothers Karamazov*. Here is greatness, holding its own.

Chapter 4

MOUNTAIN PEAKS OF
THE SUBMERGED SOCIAL
CONTINENT

T HE American Southwest is a magnetic center which draws the attention of many lands in all continents. Within my own span of contact there, these are the countries and regions whose governments, scholars, educators, artists, and workers in land-use and community-organization problems, have sought enlightenment in the American Southwest:

Scandinavia, England, Switzerland, Austria, Germany, and France; Turkey, Saudi Arabia, Palestine; China, India, and Burma, and workers with the aboriginal peoples of those lands; the British African dependencies; Greenland, New Zealand, Australia; and Mexico, Guatemala, Haiti, and the countries of the Andes in South America.

What these seekers from all over the world pursue, and find, is various, and includes all that North Americans seek and find. It includes archaeology, and the "living archaeology" of tribes whose dynamic past is moving them today; crafts and arts, and the organizational techniques of developing ancient crafts and arts to modern uses while conserving, even increasing, their traditional inspirations; the incorporation into ancient societies of modern technologies and economic, political, and legal forms; the saving of the land from water and wind erosion, a "number one" problem of our whole planet, in whose solution a number of the Southwestern tribes are leading the world; and such vistas of psychology and metapsychology as drew Carl Jung from Zurich to Taos pueblo.

Most of us Americans, and even most of those who go to observe and experience in the Southwest, are not fully aware of the unique concentration of world-wide significances found in the substance and situation of the Southwestern Indian tribes. This chapter is an endeavor to state, briefly, these significances.

Mountain Peaks of the Submerged Social Continent

A submerged social continent—the pre-white-man social continent of the whole Western Hemisphere—raises still a few mountain peaks to the sky, above the flood of change and time. Most of these peaks, and the most representative of them, are in the American Southwest.

These mountain peaks of a submerged social hemisphere heave upward through the unbroken continuity of fifteen thousand years, or longer, in North and South America. They are living social will, striving in a present from out of which this enormous past (as custom, ideal, discipline, ritual and art creation, and world view and implicit philosophy) has not died. Were the ancient Druidic civilization to be yet surviving, acting upon and reacting to the modern world from within some old oak forest of Britanny, or were the Cretan civilization of a thousand years before Christ to be gleaming today on the shores and hills of the island of Crete, the analogy with the pueblo tribes of the Southwest would be an approximate one. The confrontation of contrasts in these imagined cases—contrasts between the ancient and the contemporary—actually would be less dramatic and chasmic; for the Druid and the Cretan existed within the Aryan stream, which is our own, while the Indian tribes are of the Mongoloid stream.

Our minds are prone toward stereotypes; and one of our stereotypes is "history," conceived as a linear past gone forever; one of our stereotypes is "the present," conceived as all that moves in this instant, along this knife edge of linear time. Not thus is it possible to think realistically of the ancient-present Indians. Their past, a propulsive actuality within their social ideal and memory (a past never committed by them to books and then laid away), is immanent and enormous in their present, and is coping with the inner and outer world in behalf of a racial future.

We white men know something comparable within our own life. The Christ, veiled in an historical obscurity which no ray of historical research probably ever will illumine, simply and conclusively is not confinable within the historical stereotype at all. What history may never know, the heart and the spiritual yearning of living men do know; and the Christ is present and future. So with the Buddha, with the Socrates known through Plato's timeless dialogues, with Shakespeare, known to history only as a blind circle, known to present men as the glory and the life-shaping power of the living word.

But we modern Occidentals cannot, from within our own flow of civilization, by any stretch of our imagination, fully conceive of the dramatic situation within these ancient-present Indian tribes. To enrich our present, we go to books; there, the genius of our past is safely stored, or so we take for granted. Not ours the mighty responsibility for keeping alive, and in recurring crises renewing, the "past" of our race. These Indian tribes have no books where the genius of their past is stored; their books are languages unwritten, ritual dramas memonically conserved, initiation disciplines, songs and visual symbols, and names and meanings which unite man with heaven and earth. Nor can the human will ever cease to ply; for through ever-renewed symbolic action and intensity of inward experience—through these alone—the momentous past lives and does not die. Add to this that the Indian social groups, through whom the immense pasts must flow, are groups of few individuals, sometimes no more than one hundred, or even fewer when it is the secret societies which are the keepers and creators; and that the effort of keeping and creating is in varying degrees a collective, communal effort in which all individuals take part. And add to all of this that very real datum of a time dimension not linear, described in the opening pages of this book. Then we can at least intellectually match our minds with these Indian group minds.

But through words alone we cannot adequately tell, or adequately conceptualize, the actuality of the situation and the felt experience of these tribes in their physically small and their fleeting present and their racially vast, even cosmical, living past. That whose incorporation is only slightly realized in words, but rather in actions and non-verbal symbols and the whole deed of life, is not containable in words alone. Only physical contact with the reality, immersion in it, not from afar but out there where the tribes are, at the moments when their slow rhythms mount to maximum consciousness, can we experience what they experience. And thereafter, "words, brush and pen strive, but in vain, unto them." Let us cease, now, from the too-tenuous pursuit, and view these tribes—mountain peaks of the time-drowned continent—merely in the way that our modern Occidental mind is accustomed to view the sequences of all things, even of the soul.

White discovery and conquest dates back four hundred and fifty-seven years. Indian life in the Hemisphere dates back twelve, fifteen, or eighteen thousand years. As discovery advanced from the Eastern and Western seaboards it encountered Indian tribes or societies numbering, actually, thousands. For example, in what is now the United States alone, more than five hundred languages and dialects were spoken.

Mountain Peaks of the Submerged Social Continent

These myriads of Indian societies were exceedingly diverse, although nearly all of them had in common a certain temperament or genius which was fraught with beauty and also with fate. Columbus sensed this peculiar temperament or genius at the very beginning: a passion for rich color; extreme hospitality; a cult of giving rather than of getting, and of cooperating rather than competing; and a diffused spirituality which found God everywhere and lived in a dream of God. This was in the Caribbean islands; but Sir Francis Drake met the same qualities on the California seaboard. The Spanish chroniclers encountered these identical qualities in the dense and elaborate civilizations of Mexico and Peru; the friar Bartolomé de Las Casas described them as qualities of all Indians, and based on them his enormous, revolutionary program of Indian conversion to Christianity, and of humane statesmanship. We shall return to Las Casas and his work, because they are a living, unexhausted force in the American Southwest today.

But almost throughout the Hemisphere, the white man's actions were in extreme conflict with his initial, discerning, usually enthusiastic perceptions. Columbus kidnaped for the slave trade those islanders whose innocence and beauty he was proclaiming. He established the *encomienda* in the New World—land seized from the Indians, with the population attached as forced, practically uncompensated labor. Queen Isabella sighed and prayed over the noble red man, and enacted the code of Indian slavery and stood as the party of first interest in the traffic in slaves. The hundreds of thousands of Caribbean Indians were practically annihilated in the first thirty years after discovery.

An exploitation totally ravenous was practiced by nearly all the white invaders from the first day. Such exploitation breeds hate and scorn toward the victim; and soon the exploiting white soul perceived no longer that garden of marvelous bloom, the Indian spirit in its long summer. Instead, the white man perceived diabolism, benightedness, sloth, bloodthirstiness and racial impracticability. Secular ruthlessness was supported by religious fanaticism. The destruction of the Indian civilizations came to be an end in itself, and not only a means toward quick wealth; and there was launched the most determined, centuries-long-lasting program of social and spiritual destruction that the world has ever known.

For that record of the destruction of societies, religions, monuments, records, arts, and even technologies, this book is not the place. It continued through most of North and South America, including the United States, until a few years ago. Merely representative was the burning by the Spaniards of all the written records of Mayan Indian life which could anywhere be found; the violent subversion and extermination of the great Incaic social order, the first and last in human history to be oriented toward the intensive use of natural resources by methods of exhaustive conservation; the stamping out by our own government (after 1870) of the immense and socially creative Sun Dance religion of the Plains tribes; and the bizarre code of Indian religious crimes, enacted by the United States Indian Bureau and not repealed until 1933.

So it was, that as white exploitation advanced through centuries, the almost infinite garden of Indian life bloomed briefly before the unseeing white eye, and then was trampled down, was turned to ashes by deliberate fire.

But in the American Southwest, due to causes which we shall trace, *and almost there alone, if the arctic and subarctic north be disregarded,* the Indian life of the enormous past outwore the white centuries. The garden bloomed on, and blooms now.

So, here is the most central of the interests, the uses and "values" of Southwestern Indian life, as viewed by our cosmopolitan mind:

It reveals to us what kind of beings men were, individually and socially, in the Western Hemisphere during fifteen thousand years before the European conquest. And that revelation is a representative sampling of that which man on our earth was through a span of years nearer one hundred thousand than fifteen thousand.

It displays to us ancient man—socially, ideologically, spiritually ancient —consciously confronting all of the challenges, the problems, the influences, the desperate and as yet overmastering enigmas of our storm-shaken world in its crisis. In this, it furnishes surely one of the highest and profoundest dramas of our time; for these ancient men in their ancient societies are striving with concentrated and confident will *toward physical survival and victory only as a means to an end;* the end is spiritual survival and victory, and "spiritual" means that mystical fire which the universe, they believe, entrusted to them in a past time which must not die. The fire, they believe, even contains the inmost significance of the universe.

Their life and purpose is our world epoch in microcosm.

Chapter 5

THE NAVAJOS

FROM Albuquerque, Bill Cutter's four-passenger Fairchild roared upward into the low overcast, and pointed westward. Soon, through a cloud rift Laguana pueblo glimmered below, and then to southward Acoma pueblo on its lofty rock. Then the black land of lava flows, and northward in cloud, Mount Taylor. Beyond the Continental Divide we headed west-northwest, and we crossed the Fort Defiance plateau not a hundred feet above the tops of the high pines. How empty, the Navajo land; one lonely hogan, and no other for miles, here a herd of wild horses, there little flocks of sheep tended by children or women, then cornfields and a little village of hogans, then wasteland red as blood, where no sheep grazed. The Hopi mesas were forty miles to the west; one ray from the low winter sun illuminated the First Mesa, and Walpi tiny as a distant pebble heap. At last, circling to reconnoiter, we grounded on a sage-brush-covered mesa top, a hundred feet above the plain. We were a hundred and forty miles deep within the Navajo reservation.

Scrambling down the mesa's side, we found a car waiting, and as twilight drew near, we skidded and plunged along a road whose deep mud was not yet hardened by the night's freeze. Twenty-five miles in two hours, and then pitch-black night had come, with no stars. On the horizon, a fluctuating glow of fires, and the odor of piñon and cedar smoke drifted around us; and a low chant rising and falling, and then we were at our destination, amid wagon wheels and horses and hundreds of Navajo men, women and children. It was the fifth night of a Navajo sing.

It was Chee Dodge who had suggested our visit—Chee, who until the autumn of 1946 remained the Navajo tribal council's chairman, at eighty-seven years, and who died at the beginning of 1947. A sick Navajo woman was being healed through the sing, and Chee Dodge believed the occasion a happy one for discussing with the assembled Navajos the tribe-wide problem of the sick land. We did discuss this subject, for hours, by the wind-fanned firelight, English into Navajo, Navajo into English (for the hundreds discussed it), and all the while the chanting rose and fell from within the sick man's hogan.

And we ate mutton and drank coffee, and there was much joking and laughter while the night deepened its cold; there was happiness, although we were talking about the most painful facts and necessities which have held the Navajos in their grip in this generation.

For at a curing sing, all who attend are happy. There has taken place a disharmony, some prevalence of the dark powers which are in the world. The sing restores harmony, goes back to the sources of light, brings the reign of light; and this, not merely for the sick patient, but for all his family and friends, and not only through the medicine man's suggestion and prayer but through the union of happy emotion and confident willing on the part of every man, woman and child who has joined the ceremony. They have joined from many miles away—twenty, thirty, fifty miles. A Navajo sing is communal healing, and the sick patient throws the healing back to all who are assisting him, in a profound process of therapeutic suggestion and self-suggestion which reaches to the obscure, central deeps of the body and the soul.

There are sixty-odd thousand Navajos; theirs is the largest tribe north of Mexico. First going among them, almost anywhere in the twenty-five thousand square miles of their domain, one is impressed with the extreme material parsimony of their existence. A little patch of cornland, usually dry-farmed; twenty or thirty or fifty sheep and goats, four or five small-bodied horses. Sometimes a wagon, more rarely a decrepit car. Silver and turquoise bracelets, rings, buttons, headbands, Navajo-made, and blankets, Navajo-spun, woven and dyed, from home-grown wool; and dwellings, called hogans, windowless, built circular or octagonal of logs or stone, with dirt floors, with a vent for the fire which burns at their center, and a low doorway facing always east. Material poverty, indeed, and poverty intensifying with the years.

Such is the first impression, but the next one is sharply contrasting. It is that of vibrant human quality, body resiliency and mind resiliency, beauty of old women and young women, beauty of old and young men, poise and confidence in children, *élan* without aggressiveness in all. So poor they are; and fuller knowledge confirms and extends the first impression of material parsimony and even of a situation which realistically is desperate; and they know their situation, too, and do not try to hide it from themselves, yet the

The Navajos

note which their life strikes is exuberance and joy, a winging note and a note of the dance and the dancing star.

How can so rich a flower bloom in a soil so rocky and nearly waterless?

Out in that lonely and hard land of supernal beauty, and within their dearth of the world's goods and under the deepening shadow which rests on their future, these Navajo Indians practice a complicated art of living. Through this art, whose uninterrupted use comes down the centuries, although poverty and insecurity go on increasing, the Navajos are not poor or insecure. Thus as one's knowledge of Navajo life increases, a third impression takes form. *The Navajo has created out of his human material a house of wonder.* His intangible culture matches the splendor of his land. In terms of life, not of goods, it is we who are poor, not the Navajo.

Thus the Night Chant tells of the Navajo's house of wonder:

> House made of dawn,
> House made of evening light,
> House made of the dark cloud. . . .
> Dark cloud is at the house's door,
> The trail out of it is dark cloud,
> The zigzag lightning stands high upon it. . . .
> Happily may I walk.
> Happily, with abundant showers, may I walk.
> Happily, with abundant plants, may I walk.
> Happily, on the trail of pollen, may I walk.
> Happily may I walk.
> May it be beautiful before me.
> May it be beautiful behind me.
> May it be beautiful below me.
> May it be beautiful above me.
> May it be beautiful all around me.
> In beauty it is finished.*

The principal repositories and renewers of the Navajo's life art are his ceremonials, most but not all of them healing ceremonials. There are thirty-five major ceremonials, along with numerous variations of the thirty-five. Each requires from two to nine days for its completion, and all involve communal sharing. A full record of any one of them would require a whole book. Possibly the rite of the Blessing Way is the master ceremony of them all, because it deals with and is addressed to the universe. "A rite," explains

---

* Washington Matthews' translation.

the Franciscan Father Berard Haile, "whose legends, songs and prayers are chiefly concerned with the creation and placement of the earth and sky, sun and moon, sacred mountains and vegetation, the inner forms of these natural phenomena, the control of the he- and she-rains, dark clouds and mist, the inner forms of the cardinal points, and life phenomena that may be considered the harbingers of blessing and happiness."

Form-giving, harmony-giving, value-giving, power-giving, joy-giving, virtue-giving: the Navajo ceremonials are all of these, but these adjectives are entirely inadequate. The ceremonials are the nourishers and structurers of the Navajo personality, the expanders and ennoblers of the Navajo human relationship, the ancient renewers of Navajo civilization. Intangible as they are, yet their precision and definiteness and permanence equals that of stone or steel; immaterial as they are, yet they are potent to saturate the Navajo body and soul with a humor and dauntlessness and freedom which are all their own. Well may we of the ponderous and hurrying material civilization turn to the Navajos for a reminder that the goods of life are wrought by souls and stored within souls.

It was Changing Woman who gave to the Navajos the Blessing Way. Changing Woman is Wife to the Sun. She is the ever-renewing, ever-regenerating, ever-benign; she is Mother Earth's soul. "Seldom," writes Clyde Kluckhohn, "does a family go for six months without having the Blessing Way sung at least once in their hogan."

And what of this hogan, which to the uninitiated white visitor appears as the very concentration of the material poverty or casualness of the Navajo? Here, with a purpose, I shall draw upon another reporter of Navajo life, rather than upon my own memories. But there do come two memories, and one is from Puertocito, a remote, detached outpost of Navajo life in central New Mexico. It is night, in midwinter; a cold wind blows over a white earth under flashing stars. The hogan's diameter is twenty feet; at its center a piñon-wood fire burns. No air stirs within the hogan; the smoke rises straight to the venthole seven feet above the earthen floor.

The medicine man sits at the patient's right; the medicine man's helpers in their ordered places circle the fire. Blankets cover the floor; there are containers of liquid and powdered sacred medicines, and a silent bull-roarer is a hand. A dozen or more friend-participants are seated beyond the medicine man's helpers.

The patient is a white man; the community has contributed this sing, to

The Navajos

help him with power in a political struggle in behalf of the tribe. He notes certain facts, before the converging suggestions shepherd him within to the place where power abides. One fact is the extreme cleanliness of the firelit hogan and all within it. Another is the sweetness of the herb-scented air. Another is the orderly utilization, for storage, of every beam and cranny of the interior of the structure. The spaciousness of the place, the slow, harmonious movement of all the people in it, the gradualness of the rhythms of the ceremonial, the poised relation of unhurrying life, so quiet while at its zenith of concentration. What meanings have these words from of old, these symbolic objects from of old, the patient cannot know; but he can feel how they structure a potent, confident flow of good will and good hope. Only within a hogan can a ceremonial healing rite be performed; the hogan, the Navajo's home, is his temple too.

The other memory is of summertime, and the place, Monument Valley, at the Utah-Arizona line, northwest from Puertocito. Here, from the sand, the deep-blazing rock plinths soar to hundreds, thousands of feet. A hogan, and in front of it a spacious brush sun shelter; near by, a sheep corral. Under the brush shelter, a young woman, weaving; another young woman; and five little children of the two mothers are there. The fathers are somewhere in the Pacific theater of war. An adolescent boy is there, too; he will depart for the army next week. And the aged grandmother is there, and her aged sister; and two dogs, and a brood of kittens.

These are average Navajos, and as such, their per capita yearly income is about eighty-two dollars. No, in the barren splendor of Monument Valley the income will be lower than eighty-two dollars a year. But feeling of poverty there is none; squalor, graspingness, apology for obvious poverty, none. They smilingly accept some cookies, and offer coffee and bread to us. They bring forth letters from overseas—the two young mothers know English. They talk about the big meeting at Kayenta, twenty miles away, the day before; and will the closed government school at Kayenta be reopened soon? They joke about many things, but their jokes are in Navajo, the old and young joining in quiet laughter. But mainly their talk is concerned with a sick young man who is overstraining his family's resources by occasioning too many sings. Apparently the young man's disorder is decisively an organic one; the potent psychotherapy can dissipate its irradiations through body and mind but cannot cure the cause. But our Navajo hosts ask a subtle question: Has the young become too much Americanized? Has he ceased, when his sings are not going on, to keep to the Way? Is he doing his own part, outside the healing ceremonies? Is he running too hard after money, or girls, or drink? Or is he, perhaps, in the grip of some faithless diviner who maintains an illicit partnership with a medicine man? They do not judge, but only speculate. This troubled young man is a relative, living at the other end of the Navajo country; but these women, to whose hogan no road leads, appear to know all about the young man and his circumstances.

Here is true sophistication, and life richly lived within form; and the hogan seems enough for the abode of humans whose greater abode is Monument Valley and its shining immensities, and the whole rainbow-arched Navajo land. But now, to cite an authority on the subject of the hogan, lest my own testimony be considered overly romantic.

The authority is twofold: Clyde Kluckhohn, of Harvard University, and Dorothea Leighton, who, along with Alexander Leighton, of Cornell University, are the recognized authorities on Navajo facts. I quote from the Kluckhohn-Leighton book, *The Navaho*:

The hogan is an excellent simple adaptation to the climate: its thick walls keep out cold in winter and, to some extent, heat in summer; the centrally placed fire keeps all parts of the dwelling warm, and there is room for more occupants to sit or sleep around the fire. We (the writers) have found hogans generally more comfortable than the thin-walled cabins of white homesteaders. . . .

To the white visitor, it is astonishing how many individuals can eat, sleep, and store many of their possessions within one room not more than twenty-five feet in diameter. As a matter of fact, livable order is attained only by adherence to a considerable degree of system with respect both to objects and persons. Women always sit on the south side of the hogan, men on the north. Small children stay close to their mothers. The male head of the family and the officiating medicine men (or other distinguished visitors) sit on the west side facing the doorway. The place of other persons, and the seating arrangements under special circumstances, are prescribed in considerable detail.

Goods have a fixed disposal which utilizes all available space. Herbs and small types of dried foods, ceremonial equipment, guns and bows and arrows, hats and articles of clothing in current use, are stowed away in corners of the rafters or suspended from beams by thongs or nails. Reserve clothing and bedding, prized jewelry and ceremonial articles, are stowed in trunks or suitcases, which are stacked against the walls where the roof is lowest. Pots and pans are stacked near the central fire or placed with the spoons and supplies of flour, lard, coffee, and sugar in crude cupboards made of boxes nailed to the wall by the door. . . .

To the Navajos (Dine, The People, in their own speech), their hogans are not just places to eat and sleep, mere parts of the workaday world, as homes have tended to become in the minds of white people, particularly in cities. The hogan occupies a central

The Navajos

place in the sacred world also. The first hogans were built by the Holy People, of turquoise, white shell, jet, or abalone shell. Navajo myths prescribe the position of persons and objects within; they say why the door must always face the rising sun and why the dreaded bodies of the dead must be removed through a hole broken in the hogan wall to the north (always the direction of evil). A new hogan is often consecrated with a Blessing Way Rite or songs from it, and at the very least, the head of the family will smear the sacred corn pollen or meal along the hogan poles with some such petition as *hozhoo telgoo ot'e,* "let this be assurance that the place will be happy."

Kluckhohn's and Leighton's reference, above, to "the north, always the direction of evil," and the "dreaded bodies of the dead" occasions a remark of my own, to balance all that has gone before in this chapter. The dominant note which Navajo life strikes is joy, and buoyant confidence in the powers within the breast and in the world. And active happiness, positive health, are social duties among the Navajos. But equally, the Navajos do not enter-tain, and would scornfully reject, that view of life which is called "pan-gloss," or wilful, fact-denying, sentimental optimism. Famine, war, drought, cold, and the dark storms that are within the human soul, they have always known, and have never tried to be oblivious toward them. Darkness and evil, not only light and love and joy, are indwelling deep within the nature of things, and their attempts to invade the soul are never-ending. Once, for a long cosmic interval, gigantism and darkness and evil predominated in the whole earth; then through a mighty effort the forces of beauty, love and joy subdued them, and scattered them afar, but never annihilated or sought to annihilate them; and to man, then re-created or newly born, the Blessing Way was given, and many other symbols, precepts, rites and disciplines, and norms of conduct and feeling; and these, as lived by man, are the City of God, but darkness and active evil assail the City and invade it forevermore. Thus the cosmic and human drama is sustained by the Navajos, and the insecurity of things is wrought into a structure of beautiful security, a "dance over fire and water" whose rhythms are sometimes wildly impas-sioned but more often are stately and gradual. And in these terms, Navajo religion has its theological as well as its ethical and its aesthetic-emotional place among the fundamental religions of mankind. And Navajo religious art builds for eternity through building into the human and social tissue and soul, none the less for the fact that its material constructions are de-molished on the very day that they are completed.

These material constructions of Navajo religious art are the dry paintings or sand paintings which are created as an element of the healing ceremonies and the ceremonies which renew the occult nature-man relationship. Sand painting is a misnomer, since often, as in the paintings which are an element in the Blessing Way ceremonial, the design and color materials are pollen, corn meal of various hues, and the crushed petals of dried flowers; in the curing ceremonials the materials are charcoal and various pulverized stones. The background of the paintings usually is buckskin; sometimes it is sand.

Always the dry paintings are almost exclusively symbolic; often the design is a triumph of construction. A dry painting may be one or two feet across, or twenty feet or more, and each is the work of from two to fifteen or more ceremonial artists. A complete ceremonial requires four dry paintings, made on successive days; and always the painting is destroyed at the end of the day. The reason is not secrecy, for the Navajos have allowed more than five hundred dry paintings to be viewed and described, and a large number to be reproduced in paintings or colored photographs. Each of the five hundred recorded paintings is a precise complex of symbolism, of cosmic reference in the main; design and content have been passed down from generation to generation of healer-singers. A dry painting once perfected (and the hundreds of them were perfected in unknown times gone) may not be changed through whim or creative impulse, for it incorporates the Law from of Old. In the chants of the ceremonials, innovation and experiment have quite a free play; but the dry paintings represent creative acts of a man or group of men long dead.

It is evident, now, what is the Navajos' treasure house and what is their most priceless treasure. Treasure house and treasure are one: the scores of "ritual ways," the many hundreds of dry paintings, the thousands of songs, and the thousands of *inities* who bear in their memories these secrets of earth and heaven. Let us note, then, a rather remarkable fact.

When we look at the Navajo tribe as a whole or at any part of it, we discover that there exists no formalized or institutionalized arrangement for building their vital treasure house or for guarding the treasure house or its contents. No machinery for forcing orthodoxy or for persuading it; none for insuring that a healer-singer, before he dies, shall vest his knowledge (which is just so much of the tribe's very life) in a worthy younger man. No machinery for insuring that a younger man shall choose to become a healer-singer and shall submit himself to the years of training which will be necessary before he becomes adept. From the beginning, as now, the Navajos have entrusted their most life-and-death public function to the completely

The Navajos

unformalized and voluntary action of the aging healer-singer and of his self-elected disciples. Until now, at least, this public trust has been fully met by the old and the young; in current years, the unrecorded heritage seems to be dynamically alive and active in its entirety; the Navajos' ceremonial life is even reported by Kluckhohn and Leighton to have become intensified in the recent years.

The ready remark, certainly a superficial one, will be that healing-singing is a paid profession among the Navajos. The young man pays his healing-singing master for the years of requisite tutoring, and knows that upon graduation he will become a paid professional in his turn.

Actually, this answer does but restate the fundamentally impressive fact, that the Navajos' most important public service, the function which in the Navajo mind is life itself, is left to the free action of individuals, with no formalized or institutional provision to insure it. Of course, the healer-singer must live, therefore he must be paid. The Navajo man who is not a healer-singer devotes from one-fourth to one-third of his working time to religious activity, and the healer-singer, who also must meticulously train his successor, devotes a far greater share of his time. Among the Navajos, as among all Indians living within the ancient tribal zone, the mercenary motive is so casual, so devoid of prestige, or even so nonexistent, that no major social reliance can be placed on it alone. No, our answer must be sought elsewhere than in the concept "paid professional."

And the answer, which I shall now try to give, leads far into an understanding of many things Navajo.

The Navajos, as previously stated, are the most numerous Indian tribe north of Mexico. They also are one of the tribes with the least of centralized or even centrally-tending organization.

They possess an unmistakable community of temperament, yet their physical type is heterogeneous; they are in fact a composite of many tribal bloods.

They have adopted all sorts of culture elements from other peoples, working them over into their own Navajo pattern of culture. From the Pueblos, weaving, agricultural methods, probably even their ritual dry painting. From the Spaniards and Mexicans, the horse and sheep, and the silverwork for which Navajos are famous. From the modern United States, sundry technologies, trade practices, and notions and values which will enter into this account later on.

Indians of the Southwest

The Navajos commenced this appropriating activity at a time when they were mere single, isolated families or little groups of families, alongside the highly organized, richly cultured pueblo city-states. They continued the borrowing process through close contact with massive cultures whose quality was both definite and aggressive—Spain, and then the United States. All through these centuries they remained as they had begun, tribally inchoate; and then they became tribally subjected. Just after the American Civil War, they witnessed the destruction of all their crops, the cutting down of all their fruit trees (three thousand fruit trees in Canyon de Chelly alone), the slaughter of all their livestock, by the United States army, and were herded to exile far away, and knew that their last war had been fought and lost.

And through all these events they remained tribally inchoate, nebulous, while in their individualities and in their local communities and their religious expression they also remained uniquely and buoyantly Navajo.

Thus, at their remote Athapascan beginning, somewhere up the Rocky Mountain plateau, perhaps within Canada or interior Alaska, whatever their genius became, it became a genius diffuse, not socially concentrated. Diffuse amid scattered small groups which often, for lifetimes perhaps, had no regular contact with one another. Diffuse, without institutional form, but through some extremely impressive ancient event or some innate determination, possessed in common by that sort of vision which their Book of Genesis, the Blessing Way, communicates even to us white people with a flashing power.

In the last eighty years, they have multiplied fourfold or sixfold. As a total tribe, a supposedly unified nation, they experienced the devastating shock of violent subjugation and forced exile. In all the years after, they have been pressed by necessities and emergencies national, tribal, over-all in their character. Still they have moved ahead without an institutional, tribal structure; they have not even moved in the direction of one, except very superficially at a white political level; they have relied on that diffuse instinct and genius which has been so uniquely theirs since a date far back in the Indian Stone Age.

That genius is the shaping of glad life through a multitude of highly structured rituals never integrated into a churchly religion, never removed from out of the play of unlimited free spiritual enterprise. There was no need for integration or regulation, because the spiritual winging along the

The Navajos

old migration route of the Navajo soul was so strong and sure. Diffused vision, diffused purpose were enough; they required no centralized persuasion to insure the homing flight of the Navajo spirit, or the renewal of that flight from age to age.

Perhaps the Navajo shaman, diviner, diagnostician is a symbol of this diffuse genius of his race. The Navajo diviner is not trained in his art. He is called by the family of the sick person. Wide awake, the diviner waits. Then his arm and hand start trembling. He gropes a while, hesitating, in suspense; at length, the hand marks out on the scattered corn meal an ancient symbol. The malady is thus diagnosed, the particular healing ritual is indicated, the particular healer-singer is chosen.

We have looked at the undimmed rainbow of Navajo spiritual-aesthetic life. What sort of actualities, biological and economic, rest beneath its span?

When the Navajos were returned, in 1868, from their exile in eastern New Mexico, they numbered (including those never sent into exile) perhaps twelve thousand. They number, now, sixty thousand. They increase at two per cent a year—nearly twice as fast as the Indians of the country as a whole, more than twice as fast as the general population.

The government encouraged them—even, through indirection, compelled them—to multiply their livestock without any account taken of what amount of livestock load the range could support without being ruined. This livestock was sheep, goats, some cattle, and semi-wild horses to a maximum of two hundred thousand head at the peak of horse population.

The soil, trampled and eaten out to the roots of its vegetation, fought a rapidly losing battle. The wind blew it in dust clouds, flash floods swept it in rusty torrents toward the Colorado River, sheet erosion silently pilfered the topsoil. By the year 1933, a human population multiplied nearly fourfold since 1868 was subsisting on a land base whose potential had dwindled by more than one-half since 1868. The safe carrying capacity of the tribe's whole land area had fallen to some six hundred thousand sheep units. (A cow or horse represents four sheep units.) The sheep units on this land numbered one million three hundred thousand. That meant an erosion increasing at geometrical, not arithmetical speed; it meant near-impending doom.

At that time—May, 1933—a man who soon was to influence rural-life policy in many lands was obscurely stationed in the Department of Agriculture at Washington. His name was Hugh L. Bennett, chief of the Bureau of Soil Chemistry.

I had become Indian Commissioner, under Harold L. Ickes, who had become Secretary of the Interior. From Henry A. Wallace we borrowed Hugh L. Bennett's services. We made Bennett the chairman of a commission of forestry, range and soils specialists; the commission went to the Navajo reservation. They found, in detail, the state of facts which is summarized above.

In July, 1933, at Fort Wingate, New Mexico, Bennett made his report directly to the Navajo tribe. We had not requested its prior clearance with the Washington office. Among other dread facts suddenly unrolled before the Navajo mind, was the necessity that the livestock load on the total range should be cut in half, without delay.

The range must be saved or the Navajos must disperse into the white world. Dispersal would bring death to the Navajo spirit, the obliteration of the Navajo rainbow forever.

That meeting, July, 1933, launched a social, economic, and political struggle and effort well-nigh as intense and as dubious of outcome as any to be witnessed among men. It launched, also, the soil conservation movement of the United States; and that movement was to extend to every continent, in the years when there was dawning in the world's mind, through Hugh L. Bennett's leadership, the realization that mankind itself is faced by a silent crisis hardly less demanding than that which was facing the Navajo tribe. For the wastage of soil resource—of food potential—is going ahead on a world scale, and at an accelerating, catastrophic speed. But we will stay with the Navajos, and not enter upon the world story.

The unconcentrated, diffuse character of Navajo society has been told above. It was (and is) essentially a preliterate society, whose genius was oriented not toward organization nor toward technological achievement but toward imaginative and religious expression and the direct affirmation of buoyant life. All the years of governmental contact had not brought any tribe-wide organization into being, other than a small tribal council of very limited powers chosen by white electoral methods from large districts at infrequent elections.

The United States Government, on its side, to that date had scarcely sought to know, or to reach to, the obscure, informal, local embodiments

The Navajos

of Navajo social order—the hundreds of extended families and local communities, where the deliberative processes of the Navajos went forward in ways of ancient Indian democracy and by the method of unanimous decisions slowly arrived at.

Tribe-wide synchronized action was demanded by the facts—action painful, and also complicated; for when the stage of critical erosion has been reached, as on much of the Navajo land, soil conservation requires more, much more, than merely the reduction of livestock overpopulation. How, when tribe-wide organization did not exist, could tribe-wide action, rapid, painful and complicated, be insured?

We in the Indian Service in 1933 knew that this enigma had three possible answers.

The first of the answers was: Direct compulsion by the government. The legal authority existed; and compulsion had been the traditional method of the Indian Service toward all Indians for eighty years.

The second of the answers was: To throw the whole staggering responsibility onto the Navajo Tribal Council—onto the almost phantom-frail political institution of the tribe. This choice would mean using federal governmental authority, if at all, solely to the end of carrying out requests or ordinances of the Tribal Council.

The third answer was: Go with the facts to the hundreds of local communities of the Navajo people. Educate these communities through slow, patient conference and demonstration. Vest the responsibility for launching and guiding these huge, necessary adjustments, in the local headmen, in the healer-singers, the diviners, and ultimately, the heads of families.

We rejected the third of the choices because that ideal method was beyond our practical power, or because we believed it was beyond our practical power. In this rejection we may have erred profoundly; I shall touch upon that question later in this text.

We chose the second answer. We threw the burden squarely onto the Navajo Tribal Council. And the Council lifted the burden.

Then there commenced a political event rare if not unique in the history of popular government. The Council accepted and affirmed the conservation program, with its bitter requirement of a slashing stock reduction, because its intellect and conscience required it to. The Council's constituency did not accept the program, but resisted it with a bitterness sometimes sad, sometimes angry and wild. The Council stood firm, and the electorate threw it out of office. The successor Councilmen, confronting the implacable facts, reaffirmed and extended the conservation program, including the stock reductions. The electorate threw this successor Council out of office; and again the new Council affirmed the program and extended it. Thus, onward for ten years.

Not often do legislators, in the absence of corporation or big-money or other pressure-group influence, deliver themselves for electoral slaughter by going counter to the impassioned, even inflamed will of the vast majority of their constituents. That is what the Navajo legislators did. They did it under no sort of duress and bribery of the Indian Service; duress and bribery were not possible and were not attempted. They did it out of political virtue of a high order, and under no compulsion except that of an overwhelming reality which they acknowledged after they entered on responsibility. They were helpless to communicate their understanding to the mass of the Navajos; but upward along the line of greatest unpopularity, greatest resistance, the Navajo Council moved.

The needful stock reductions have been practically completed now; the animal load is yielding a greater total value of meat and wool than the greater number of animals were yielding ten years ago. This, because of upbreeding, improved water supply, removal of surplus horses which were consuming the grass in the earlier years, and, in some parts of Navajo land, a healing and revegetation of the wounded range. The result has been paid for by anguish of spirit among most of the Navajos, extreme material hardship among thousands of them, and a truncating of the tribe's political development. The burden cast on the frail Tribal Council, and so bravely carried by it, was a burden too great. The disunion between the Council and the basic Navajo social order was altered, through the conservation struggle, from one of mere non-connection to one of resentment, fear, and active resistance.

Was, therefore, our choice made in 1933 a wrong choice? Should we in this one case have utilized sheer, direct authority, by-passing the Navajos' immature political institution and thus sparing it? Or should we, as the alternative, have depended solely on persuasion and education at the "grass roots"—in the many local communities?

In the whole retrospect, I answer that our choice was not wrong. As a basic policy, we had terminated the use of coercion upon Indian tribes. We could not, in the affairs of the largest tribe and in the most poignant of its issues, reinstitute coercion; for that would have been to betray the cause of all Indians. It was right to cast the burden on the Navajos' elected agents; these agents knew that it was right.

Our error was in another direction, and I dwell upon it briefly because it is the continuing error of the Navajo sector of Indian Service.

We could not, or did not, move the conservation problem through and beyond the centralized political organ of the tribe, out to the local communities where the Navajos' real profundities and strengths have their abode. In the same way, we did not move the Navajos' health problems out there; and their schooling and adult education problems; and all of their other problems, and Indian administration itself.

There were many other reasons, other than deficiency of effort, for this failure; they almost aggregated to impossibilities; there are many reasons why the failure continues still; and this text is not the place to discuss the intricacies of Indian Service budgeting, personnel, and institutionalism, the limitations placed in appropriation acts by Congressional prejudice and whim, the "pump priming" requirements of the depression years which compelled the spending of public monies at extreme speed. The idiosyncrasies of United States federal administration are not the subject of this book. But with the destiny of the Navajos, and their crisis, still unresolved, and their future, not yet spelled out, every reader will be concerned. I shall describe briefly this Navajo crisis of today, at the cost of some slight repetition. It exists in two aspects, inseparable from each other: the Navajo aspect, and the United States governmental aspect.

Immense effort, and much pain, across nearly sixteen years, has reversed the soil-wastage process on most of that part of the Navajos' land which had not been incurably wrecked before 1933. And, as stated above, the greatly diminished livestock load is returning larger money values than did the nearly one hundred per cent overload of fourteen years ago. Yet today, viewing the Navajo domain in its entirety, we find that one single sheep requires thirty acres for its browse. And we find that the entire livestock yield (meat and wool sold and consumed) supplies no more than 44 per cent of the average per capita yearly income of the Navajos; and the total per capita income is only $82. Farming accounts for 14 per cent of the total income; arts and crafts, 11 per cent; and wages for government and private labor, 30 per cent. Compare this Navajo per capita income with other (pre-World War II) per capitas: the United States as a whole, $597;

Indians of the Southwest

Arizona, $473; New Mexico, $359; and the State of lowest income in the Union, Mississippi, $205. Two items are added, as annotation. The Navajo pays all the federal taxes and most of the state taxes except the land tax, which for people of low incomes, in New Mexico and Arizona, is negligible anyway. He receives free schooling for about one-third of his children, and free medical service for a fraction of his population not larger than one-fourth. He gets few of the social-security benefits which the non-Indians in New Mexico and Arizona receive. If anyone has the idea that Navajos, and other Indians, "live off of the government," or that Indian Service receives too much appropriated money, let him consider the items here set down.

Is this material poverty of the Navajos a fixed fact? No; for given the necessary capital, given administrative wisdom, and given time, the unused potentials of the country and also of the people can be brought alive. The irrigated farmland can be increased from 23,000 acres to more than 120,000. The per acre yield of farmland certainly can be doubled. With continued upbreeding of the livestock and continued revegetation of the damaged range, livestock income can be doubled in the generation ahead. The large timber wealth of the tribe can be manufactured into furniture, not merely cut into boards. The Navajo reservation contains many billion tons of accessible coal; and there is helium, and other minerals. The market demand for fine-quality Navajo blanket and silver and turquoise work is insatiable; here, the potential increase of Navajo income is indefinite. Payment of government wages to whites, and to Indians other than Navajos, in the Navajo Indian Service, totals some hundreds of thousands of dollars a year; and within a reoriented program and administrative system, most of this payment could go to Navajos.

Clearly, Navajo material poverty *is not* a fixed fact.

Wherein, then, rests the "crisis still unresolved," the "future not yet spelled out"?

First, and most obvious: Navajo population is not a fixed fact. Increase is at the rate of two per cent a year. Population is snowballing, as it has done since the Navajos' return from exile in 1868. Writes Clyde Kluckhohn: "There can be no doubt that the fecundity of the tribe is but one symptom of a generally radiant vitality. They want to live. They want children, many children." Let the Navajo death rate be brought down to that of the Indians of the country as a whole, and the population rise will approach three per cent, not two per cent, a year.

The Navajos

Second, and nearly as obvious: Many thousands of Navajos, women as well as men, through the war years were in the armed forces or in war industry. They became used to a material "standard of living" perhaps seven times higher than the average of their homeland. They became used to substituting this richer material standard for that very rich communal spiritual standard which no material poverty can dismay.

But unless the fullest of employment levels is maintained in the country, these Navajos will not be preferred in industry. With but few exceptions indeed, their rhythms are not those which industry requires; they will be viewed as a marginal labor supply. They will stay at home, entertaining material wants which the home world cannot supply now. Within a Navajo economic program wisely conceived and early launched, these returned veterans and war workers could be a decisive factor in terms of equipment, energy and ambition. Wanting that program (at this writing, 1949, it is still wanting), even the deep potency of the Navajo healing and reconciling ceremonials may not be enough to assuage them. They are one of their people's resources now; they can become its most troublesome disrupter and destroyer.

The really deep, controlling aspect of the Navajos' crisis has yet to be told. Population increase, and tensions brought home from the war and war industry, are among the precipitators of this deep and controlling aspect of the crisis, but they are not the essential part of it.

The deep, controlling crisis of Navajo life is found in the relationship between the United States Government and the Navajos. It is a crisis in Navajo Indian administration.

The main burden of this chapter has been to show where it is that the life treasure of the Navajos lies. It lies in the family and extended family, the local community, the headman who holds power only through democratic leadership, and the religious functioning—the healer-singer and his many helpers, the diviner, the wondrous ceremonials, the union of faith and prayer in joy, the many cooperative commonwealths of souls. Here, personality is formed, values and life attitudes are established, self-discipline, and that gallant buoyancy of spirit, that "radiancy" of the Navajo being, are communicated from man to man and from the elder to the younger generation.

Here the genius, the very existence of the Navajo is found. Here is no exclusiveness, but universal hospitality; no fear of new things or of change, since during hundreds of years the Navajos have changed and changed and changed again, have adopted new arts, new technologies, new industries, and have changed not at all at this life-generating core of their society.

And now, it must be added: Indian Service never has brought to bear the patience, perseverance, will and art needed to connect itself and its programs with the local complexes which really *are* the civilization and society of the Navajo. Hardly has it even tried factually to equate its programs with these basic Navajo facts.

Blind or hostile toward the Navajos' deep powers in their local embodiments, Indian Service has not been, at least not within recent years. But Indian Service has trafficked with Navajo individuals, and with Navajo electoral masses, in terms of this or that or the other program or service, without even trying, seriously, to communicate with the controlling sources of Navajo opinion, responsibility, power and genius. White personnel, Indian personnel from Oklahoma and the Great Plains and Lake States, few of them speaking the Navajo language, have received their Navajo Service assignments, brief or not quite so brief, and then have wended their way to other regions of Indian country, to be succeeded by newcomers who would prove to be as transitory as themselves. And always (as in the conservation effort recounted in this chapter), to those in charge of services and programs, it has seemed that there was not time enough to deal with the fundamental leadership among the Navajos, and with the local communities, and with the controlling intangibles of Navajo existence.

In earlier years, it did not matter very seriously that the government and its programs had not even a speaking acquaintance with the real centers of Navajo opinion and power. The programs were extremely circumscribed, and the great body of Navajo life remained untouched by them. But after 1933 the totality of Navajo existence became affected by the conservation program. And in the years now ahead, if the Navajos' economic crisis is to be met, the actions in the first instance must be governmental, and their consequences will reach through all of Navajo life. The continuing chasm between government Indian Service and the creative, responsible, potent parts of Navajo society therefore matters, now, very seriously indeed.

To make the above statement in another way. Are Navajos to do their own work, including the making of their own deliberative decisions? Are those of the Navajo people who have prestige, responsibility, wisdom, and leadership to be utilized in meeting a tribal crisis which plainly is a fateful one? Are the Navajos' social and spiritual energies and values to become harnessed for the great, difficult tasks ahead, or are these energies and values to be by-passed, dispensed with, kept in an outer darkness? The answer to these questions contains the very fate of the Navajos—certainly their spiritual, probably also their physical, fate.

How the question is answered will be of profound interest to workers throughout the colonial, preliterate, preindustrial world.

The right—the saving—answer will require of the Indian Service central headquarters a reoriented creativeness. It will lay that requirement intensely on the Navajo field service personnel. The saving answer will lead far and deep in ways of the good.

Chapter 6

THE PUEBLOS

WHEREVER, in the two Americas, the white explorer, conqueror or missionary went, he encountered Indian civilizations. Many hundreds of volumes, published and unpublished, of letters, reports and chronicles, depict his first impressions and recount his own actions.

Today, wherever a visitor penetrates the Americas, except in the far north and a few tropical regions, he no more sees that which the explorers saw. Be it Massachusetts, Virginia or Florida, California or the Candian west coast, Mexico, the Caribbean, Central America, the Andes, Chile, Argentina: the Indian civilizations are gone, or are profoundly changed, and the change nearly always has been retrogressive or disintegrative; and often there are no more Indians at all, where once the white man encountered them in every land.

The exception is the Pueblo tribes of New Mexico and Arizona. Here, Coronado and his "many gentlemen" came in 1540; "the most brilliant company ever collected in the Indies to go in search of new lands," as the humble Pedro de Casteñada, one of their company, and their chronicler, describes them. From Casteñada's pages of excellent and sympathetic description one can step right into the Pueblos of today. Were Casteñada to return from the dead as one's guide, he would make note of changes, indeed, but not of changes which have altered the rhythms which he experienced four centuries ago, or the social manners, or the religions in their deeps, or the social organizations at their centers.

Changes there have been, some of them quite radical. No longer do the men live year long in the kivas (the underground ceremonial houses, headquarters of the secret societies). Husbands live with their wives and children now. No longer do the virgins move through the plazas clothed in nothing but their naked beauty. There are horses now, which there were not then, and sheep, and sometimes cattle. Through all of the New Mexico pueblos, the Christian religion long ago became incorporated as a secondary religion, without replacing or subordinating the primary religion which is central, controlling, now as of old. But in relation to the totality of Pueblo life, the changes which four hundred years have brought are by far fewer and less deep than those, for example, which the last century and a quarter have brought to the totality of life in England.

Indeed, we shall note in the Pueblos an operation which brings about an organic continuity hardly discoverable in any white or white-dominated nation or society of present times. It is an operation—conscious, complex, institutional—of keeping the past alive because the past (to the Pueblo mind) is not past but present; and not of resisting change, but of so adjusting all innovation and change that the novelty shall be at home within the imperious, creative past; and this past, within which the new change already has become ancient, moves with deep will toward a future of the tribal spirit and personality, which is meant to be endless.

I give three examples of the Pueblo attitude toward innovation and the processes of innovation.

With Christianity, in the Rio Grande pueblos, came the morality and custom of indissoluble marriage. It was a radical innovation, and apparently was welcomed by the males because it increased their status and power: the male no longer dwelt in the kiva, but lived in his children's home as co-head of the establishment. The absolute prohibition of divorce became a custom, guarded as such by the officials and priests of the ancient Pueblo religions. In recent years, repeated efforts have been made to mitigate the absoluteness of this prohibition of divorce. At Santo Domingo, in many ways the representative pueblo among those on the Rio Grande, the answer always has been: Absolute monogamy is our ancient custom, and must not be altered.

At this same Santo Domingo, a number of years ago, there arose a deadlock between the ancient religion, which largely is in the keeping of the secret societies, and a Roman Catholic archbishop, who was beloved but who was troubled over the subject of doctrinal consistency. The rule of religious secrecy, at Santo Domingo, is inviolable, hence the Christian confessional has never been admitted into the Pueblo's life. The Archbishop insisted that the Santo Domingans should confess; they politely declined, as their forbears had done ever since Christianity was embraced by the tribe. Thereupon the Archbishop withdrew all Christian services; in effect, he excommunicated the Santo Domingans.

But Christianity—the parts of it they had incorporated into their life—

was a value which the Pueblo would not consider giving up or even momentarily suspending. In the Christian church built and every year renewed by communal labor, the Christian services went forward unchanged: Latin recitative, and every element of the Christian ceremony. Only, in place of ordained white priests, it was unordained Indians who conducted the services. The difference was composed after several years; white priests renewed their services; and Santo Domingo does not confess.

At Bluebird, seven miles southward from the Hopi First Mesa, three years ago I talked through long hours with one of the Hopi old men. A spring, in the desert, waters three or four acres at Bluebird. No drop is wasted in the exquisitely terraced gardens and orchards. Flowers bloomed all about the family's home. Near by, in a large and clean cage, a ceremonial eagle awaited release, when with many messages he would be set free to return to the place of the gods.

The old Hopi man told in spacious words, with slow and precise concentric gestures, how the Hopis lived—they had always lived—in preparation and expectation for the coming of the White Brother. When that White Brother truly should come (he had not truly or fully come as yet), then all that was great and old in Hopi life would unite with all that was great and old in the White Brother's life; and the two lives would move into a future more bright, and also everlasting, neither life engulfing the other, but "like the two distinct strands woven into a single lariat."

What is the Pueblo "strand" like, which the years even now are weaving into the White-Indian "lariat"?

When Coronado pursued the phantom of gold across the American Southwest, he traversed a land of ancient civilizations. Pueblo material culture, as known to archaeology, was perhaps two thousand years old when Coronado came. Pueblo social and spiritual culture was much older—older by many thousand years. Yes, older by tens of thousands of years. View a Pueblo deer dancer of today. Then view the painting of the Sorcerer, in the night-filled Caverne des Trois Frères, in France. That painting is twenty thousand years old. The spirit and meaning of the two images is so consanguineous as to be practically identical. The spiritual culture of the Pueblos is as old as mankind on our earth. Experiencing the Shalako ceremony at Zuñi pueblo, one is brought into immediate contact with that which Sollas, in *Ancient Hunters,* calls "the symbol-steeped mind of Paleolithic man." Those clowns at the Shalako, those "mudheads," those Ne'-we-kwe, potent

The Pueblos

healers and cosmic comedians, who, almost wholly naked, move through the slow hours in zero temperature with never a shudder of cold: their medicinal power is great, their traditional wisdom is believed even greater, and their organization is very ancient; the Zuñis place its origin at the beginning of things.

"In the lost Eden of the human heart, an ancient tree of knowledge grows wherefrom the mind has not yet gathered more than a few windfalls." These words of Fiona Macleod furnish an image for the profounder meaning of the Pueblos to themselves and also to us. We on the knife edge of Occidental linear time can gather but few windfalls indeed from the "ancient tree of knowledge growing in the human heart." The Pueblos know and keep the windfalls of many ages, even back to the Dawn man. Beautiful windfalls, and nearly always good, loving, chaste and wise, and united with practical living, and valid (so the Pueblos affirm and intend) for the future life of man.

Societies organized, societies travailing and availing, in behalf of the dream of Keats in his fairest vision: "The same that oft-times hath Charm'd magic casements, opening on the foam Of perilous seas, in faery lands forlorn." But always the hallowing magic, in the Pueblo communal creation, is close to work, and to every day, and to duty, and to the shaping of a whole life. The communal weaver of souls weaves on, from the old Stone Age and within and across our own time. Here, surely, are profound meanings, and things that our present world needs, though it may not be able to take them.

Archaeological record shows the Pueblos as having been the basket-making peoples of two thousand years ago. The Basket Makers presumably spoke a number of widely dissimilar languages, as the Pueblos do now. Not until 400 A.D. did they invent pottery or acquire it from some other culture area. About 500 A.D. they received maize; it came to them from Mexico, probably by the route of the Mississippi Valley. Soon thereafter they acquired the squash and bean, and the bean furnished the essential protein content of food, which previously only wild game had furnished.

Possessing corn and beans, the Basket Makers could cease to wander. They dug pits in the earth to store their corn; then they built storage rooms of rock, above ground. Then, after their cliff-dwelling stage, they built their towns—communal fortress dwellings rising five and six stories high. Their city-state societies developed to structural complication and to a high degree of integration. Their land area (not all of it simultaneously occupied) was a far-flung one, reaching south into what is now Mexico, northward far into what are now Nevada and Utah, into southern Colorado, and through most of Arizona and New Mexico.

Our chronology of Pueblo prehistory is a very exact one, thanks to the work of A. E. Douglass on tree rings. A tree three hundred years old records in its rings the rainfall record of three centuries. Wet years, wide rings; dry years, narrow rings. Local rainfall variations enter this record, but also, cycles of rain abundance and of drought which are region-wide.

Tree-ring chronology works backward from the oldest living tree which can be found. Then a log or beam from some early structure built within historical times is examined; the rings at the center of the living tree will overlap with those at the periphery of the tree cut so many hundred years ago. Then the ring record of a yet older beam is overlapped with the more recent one, and so on back, until now we have an unbroken ring chronology to the year 11 A.D.

Thus, any ruin with wood in it of substantial size can be dated in terms of the master chart of tree rings. Ruins with no wood are dated by comparing the objects found in them with those from ruins dated by the tree-ring calendar.

It is through tree-ring dating that we know when Old Oraibi, on the Hopi Third Mesa, was built. The date was about 1100 A.D. But the Hopis were an ancient people before the first stone and beam of Old Oraibi were laid. And now, when Old Oraibi crumbles away and few of the living are within its thousand-year-old homes and the Hopi spirit has grown weary there and seems to look only toward the past, others of the Hopi city-states are as young in their ancientness as they were a millennium or two millennia ago, and are confronting enigmas which appear almost unconquerable, with no fear.

Let us go back four hundred years, and see the Pueblos as the first white men to enter the Southwest saw them; also, the first white men as these men appeared to the Pueblos. Pedro de Casteñada's narrative is our source.

Spain had conquered Mexico in 1520, and Peru in 1532. Each conquest had yielded enormous wealth of gold and silver. But the Spanish crown was insatiable, and the adventurers in the New World lived in a delirious dream of gold. A mere fable or "hunch" that gold existed in some new direction sufficed to insure a new expedition, heroic and ruthless, and usually ruinous to the native inhabitants of jungle, island, mountain or desert. Thus Zuñi

The Pueblos

pueblo became the goal of Coronado's expedition: "the Seven Cities of Cibola," gleaming with gold.

Coronado found no gold at Zuñi, nor at Tusayan (the Hopi pueblos), nor at Acoma, or the Rio Grande pueblos, or Pecos pueblo, east of the present Santa Fe, now extinct. But at Pecos he found an Indian of some tribe far eastward. This Indian is designated in the chronicle as the "Turk." He could communicate only by signs, but to this effect the enamored Spaniards understood him:

There was an Eldorado, many weeks' journey to the east. A river two leagues wide, and the fishes in it were big as horses, and mighty canoes, with twenty rowers on each side, and with sails, plied the river, and the lords of the country sat on the poops under awnings, and on the prows were great eagles of solid gold. And the chief lord of that Eldorado took his afternoon nap under a great tree on which were hung a great number of little gold bells, which put him to sleep as they swung in the air. Everyone in that Eldorado had his ordinary dishes made of wrought gold; and the jugs and bowls were of gold.

So, led by the Turk, and led circuitously, because their prisoner-guide was seeking to lose them in some waterless waste, Coronado and his numerous entourage journeyed eastward on the Great Plains. Their destination was the Wichita tribe of what is now eastern Kansas, called by the Turk the Quivira. The Wichitas, of course, proved to have no gold, whereupon Coronado garroted the Turk. Casteñada thus describes the marvelous vegetation of the Plains, as it remained after millennia of Indian use and as it is no more:

Who could believe that 1,000 horses, and 500 of our cows, and more than 5,000 rams and ewes and more than 1,500 friendly Indians and servants, in travelling over these plains, would leave no more trace where they had passed than if nothing had been there —nothing—so that it was necessary to make piles of bones and buffalo-dung now and then, so that the rear guard could follow the army. The grass never failed to become erect after it had been trodden down, and, although it was short, it was as fresh and straight as before.

But we are digressing from Casteñada's observations of the Pueblos, and Coronado's actions there.

Cicuye [Pecos] is a village of nearly five hundred warriors. It is a square, situated on a rock, with a large court or yard in the middle, containing the estufas [kivas, underground ceremonial houses and headquarters of the secret societies]. The houses are all alike, four stories high. One can go over the top of the whole village without there being a street to hinder. There are corridors going all around it at the first two stories, by which one can go around the whole village. These are like outside balconies, and they are able to protect themselves under these. The houses do not have doors below, but they use ladders, which can be lifted up like a drawbridge, and so go up to the corridors which are inside the village. There is a spring of water inside, which they are able to divert.

Cibola [Zuñi] is seven villages. The houses are ordinarily three or four stories high, but in Macaque [then the largest Zuñi town, now a ruin] there are houses with four and seven stories. These people are very intelligent. They cover their privy parts and all the immodest parts with cloths made like a sort of table napkin, with fringed edges and a tassel on each corner, which they tie over the hips. They wear long robes of feathers and of the skins of hares, and cotton blankets. The women wear blankets, which they tie or knot over the left shoulder, leaving the right arm out [exactly as now, 1949, at Zuñi]. They [the women] gather their hair over their two ears, making a frame which looks like an old-fashioned headdress. [The Hopi maidens still wear their hair thus.]

They do not have chiefs, as in New Spain [Mexico], but are ruled by a council of the oldest men. They have priests who preach to them, whom they call papas [in Zuñi, meaning Elder Brothers]. These are the elders. They go up on the highest roof of the village and preach from there, like public criers, in the morning while the sun is rising, the whole village being silent and sitting in the galleries to listen [as now, at Taos, for example]. They tell the pople how they are to live, and I believe that they give certain commandments for them to keep, for there is no drunkenness among them nor sodomy nor sacrifices, neither do they eat human flesh or steal, but they are usually at work.

The young men [of the Tiguan or Tanoan pueblos along the Rio Grande] live in the estufas [kivas]. They are underground, square or round, with pine pillars. Some were seen with twelve pillars, and with four in the center as large as two men could stretch around. Some estufas that were seen were large enough for a game of ball. . . . When any man wishes to marry, it has to be arranged through those who govern. The man has to spin and weave a blanket, and place it before the woman, who covers herself with it and becomes his wife [as now in the Hopi Pueblos].

The villages are free from nuisances, because they go outside to excrete, and they pass their water into clay vessels, which they empty at a distance from the village [as now]. They have separate houses [rooms within the great houses] where they prepare the food for eating and where they grind the meal, very clean. In this separate room they have a trough with three stones fixed in stiff clay. Three women go in there, each one having a stone, with which one of them breaks the corn, the next grinds it, and the third grinds it again. They take off their shoes, do up their hair, shake their clothes, and cover their heads, before they enter the door. A man sits at the door playing on a fife while they grind, moving the stones to the music and singing together. [The corn-grinding song can still be heard in most of the pueblos.]

In *Indians of the Americas,* I remarked that Coronado was perhaps the gentlest of all the many *conquistadores* who went into the New World from

The Pueblos

Spain. His journey in the American Southwest preceded by just a year the promulgation of the humanitarian New Laws of the Indies by the King of Spain—laws largely written by Bartolomé de Las Casas; and his journey was commenced soon after the infamous Nuño de Guzman, in Mexico, had received dire punishment for bloody outrages committed upon the Indians. On the whole, the judgment was accurate: Coronado in his actions was the gentlest of the *conquistadores*. But the incident now to be told suggests that the difference lay in circumstances, not in character. Since he found no gold among the Pueblos, Coronado did not expect to stay there. Meantime, he depended on the Pueblos for subsistence and even for clothing; his new concentration was on the phantom of gold at Quivira, to which the half-mad Indian, the Turk, was leading him on. This is the incident the memory of which was to remain with the Pueblos for centuries after:

At Pecos, Coronado kidnaped two of his kindly hosts, the kidnaped men being priestly headmen. Thereafter, holding these men prisoner, he wintered with the Tiguex Pueblos, on the Rio Grande, during the winter of 1540-41. The Tiguex (pronounced Tee-guaysh) Pueblos were that Tanoan group whose representatives today are Isleta, Sandia, Picuris and Taos. These Pueblos were troubled at the violence done their neighbor, Pecos pueblo.

Nevertheless, hospitality being their law, then as it is now, they shared what they had with the Spaniards. Coronado requested large gifts of clothing for his men. The Pueblos acceded, but explained that the levy of clothing in the twelve villages (there were then that number) must be in the hands of the authorities of each village.

But Coronado and his men would not wait; they raided the villages and seized whatever clothing they desired, even stripping many of the Indians practically naked.

Then one of Coronado's men attempted to rape a Pueblo woman. The woman's husband brought the facts to Coronado, but the offender remained unpunished.

Then the villages went defensively "on the warpath." They shut the Spaniards out. Coronado concentrated his forces against the village where the attempt at rape had occurred. There was bloody but indecisive fighting; then the Spaniards invited the village to make peace, assuring it that there would be no reprisals. The village made peace, and its warriors delivered themselves into the Spaniards' hands.

But Coronado had directed his captain, Don Garcia, to take no man of the village alive. Calmly, Don Garcia ordered that two hundred stakes be erected and that every warrior be burned alive. "Then," recites Casteñada, "when the Indians saw that the Spaniards were binding them and beginning to roast them, about a hundred men who were in the tent began to struggle and defend themselves with what was there and with the stakes they could seize. Our men who were on foot attacked the tent on all sides, so that there was great confusion around it, and then the horsemen chased those who escaped. As the country was level, not a man of them remained alive, unless it was some who remained hidden in the village and escaped that night to spread throughout the country the news that the strangers did not respect the peace they had made, which afterward proved to be a great misfortune."

Casteñada does not record that Coronado ever reprimanded his too-literally-obedient captain.

It was not until a hundred and forty years later that the Pueblos exacted their full, if temporary, revenge for this incident and many like incidents at the hands of successor *conquistadores*—among these incidents being the *semana,* New Granada's name for Spain's *repartimiento,* or uncompensated forced-labor system, which blighted and depopulated much of the New World. In 1680, the Pueblos, led by Taos pueblo, united, and killed or drove out from New Granada the last Spaniard. They were reconquered after eight years; but here, at the margin of her empire, Spain finally made operative almost the whole policy of Bartolomé de Las Casas. Pueblo policy became the fine flower of the realized Laws of the Indies; and over the long span it can be said that Spain allowed the Pueblo civilizations to live into our modern day. Will we allow them to live into a day beyond our own? This question is not yet answered. I shall try to make credible and understandable the suggestion that the question is not a little but a big one—that its Yes or No answer can have consequences for our nation and world.

First, let us view the Pueblos from a few of the many angles and levels which invite inspection.

They are communities based on agriculture. They have existed and evolved through a very long time. Agriculture is nothing less than a fine art with them—the more impressively so as one moves to arid Hopiland.

As agricultural communities, they deal with the land—its soil, water, vegetation and wild life—not in the spirit of exploitation but in the spirit of reciprocity. A better word than reciprocity is brotherhood—active, con-

The Pueblos

siderate, loving brotherhood. This means that they are conservationists; and present years are demonstrating that their conservation-mindedness is ready to take and use all of the applicable modern technologies of conservation. By ancient tradition, and with imaginative intensity, and within the slow, un-failing rhythms which they have taken from nature and made into their own social and spiritual rhythms, they function as *applied ecologists*. They have functioned thus for fifteen centuries or longer in the prescientific way of in-tuition and accumulated experience. When, as at Acoma pueblo, since 1936, they add to their prescientific ecology the modern technologies and organiza-tional techniques, they are not aware of incompatibility or conflict between the two orders. The white man assumes that such incompatibility exists and that it dooms the prescientific, mystic, religious, aesthetic, intuitional world view and sentiments and complexes. The Pueblo Indian silently repudiates that assumption. The livingness of the earth, the reality of the two-way flow between earth and man, the deeply religious character of that relationship, are the fundamental premise of Pueblo life. New technologies, including the mathematical and quantitative operations of science, *if they be ecologically relevant and true within the Pueblo environment,* are brought into the ancient ecological enterprise and institution without collision or contra-diction.

The Pueblos already have achieved brilliantly as ecological conservationists in the modern way. But if the assertion in the paragraph above be true—as it certainly is true—it follows that achievement more brilliant and more pro-found is ahead, or can be ahead. Nature works toward ecological harmony, mutuality—and toward what Ward Shepard has called the ecological climax-type. When man works with, instead of against, this silent, multitudinous ecological creativeness of nature, then man in his inner nature and in his society becomes an active, harmonious portion and partner in the ecological creation. He becomes united with the cosmos, self-shaped into the image of the Mighty Brother, the Mighty Mother, the Earth Mother whose prodigal and recreant son modern exploitative man has come to be. And he becomes psychically and socially stabilized within a living freedom.

The issue here is nothing less than that of lasting world peace, of the new epoch of peace within the heart, of society-nature morality, of reasserted ecological intent, and of creative living on the part of all men, which *must dawn* if man and men and earth are to go on existing together.

The Pueblos are statistically small—there are approximately the same number of Pueblo Indians as there were of free citizens of ancient Athens. The Rochdale cooperative institution in England a hundred years ago was small—its members numbered twenty-eight. Switzerland is small—yet it has demonstrated across centuries the right relation between local community and central government, and the practicability of multilingual cultural pluralism within a political nation stable and integrated. Many a "voice in the wilderness" has become the voice of multitudes and of races in the short span of written history; indeed, few other voices than those which were lonely voices at the creative beginning have ever become the lasting voices of multitudes and races. Statistical size does not measure social, spiritual, aesthetic, philosophical potency, value or future. Structural significance and applicability are the measures of these things; moral magnitude is their measure; and relevancy to the nature and the necessities of man in the long run. And statistical smallness joined with lastingness through time is usually the precise condition necessary for profound social achievement which the mass society shall thereafter appropriate.

Peculiarly potent in achievement is the small social group whose members are moved by ideas of universal character and intention, and whose situation is representative of that of great masses or of the whole race. Thus were the Rochdale cooperative pioneers of the 1840's situated. How could the poorest men of industrial England, who had no society of their own any more, and no freedom and no power—how could they have a society anew, and freedom and power in and through it? The universal question echoed from land to land, the social institution of distributive cooperation, which these obscure men invented as the answer, became naturalized in land after land.

The Pueblos, I suggest, in their philosophy and practice of the man-nature relationship, and in their ecological practice which makes of the human society a co-operant part of the planetary and cosmical ecological creation, are the askers of a question and the propounders of an answer even more universal than were the question and answer of Rochdale. The question and answer of the Pueblos ring like bells in the heart of every human child, and ring like bells muffled by many veils and almost drowned in many noises, yet audible, in the forsworn deeps of the adults of our epoch which is rushing to its terminus. They tell that happy man, unwounded earth, and long, endless future can be had by our race still.

Such is one view of the Pueblos, from one of the many angles. I now suggest some other views, from other angles.

The Pueblos

I offer this remark, first, that every phase or part of Pueblo life, if examined patiently, is found to lead to all the other parts, and to involve them. Pueblo life is complicated and is almost uniquely many-sided, while at the same time its integration is so complete and profound that every particular item or expression is found to involve, and to be involved with, all the rest of the many-sided complication. This interrelatedness of all the parts is not a matter of mere physical proximities or of formalized prearrangements; rather, it is like the interrelatedness of the organs and cells of a living being, and it suggests that unique goal-seekingness and striving-togetherness of all the organs and functions of a living body, which is the distinguishing character and the ultimate mystery of organic life.

In Pueblo societies, the analogue of the central nervous system and the hormones and vitamins (the principal integrating mechanisms in organisms) appears to be the *symbol system,* which exists and produces its effects above the threshold of consciousness and also beneath it. This symbol system conserves from very ancient times the world view of the Pueblo, the orientations and values that are essential to Pueblo life, the intuitively held philosophy of the Pueblo, and the *whither* of Pueblo destiny. The symbol system of no Pueblo is completely known to science as yet; still less is the symbol system of any Pueblo fully understood in terms of its origins and of its dynamical effects within the Pueblo individual and Pueblo society. But enough is known to confront the student of human life with an invitation to further study, and the invitation is as exciting as any to be met in the science and philosophy of man. Here, we are close to that in man and man's society which is uniquely human, which is the creative factor in human history, and which prophesies the spiritual nature of man in future millenniums.

I dare not try, and am not equipped, to pursue in this text the enormous subject of the role of symbol systems as the conservers and propellers of the deep life of man, the definers and molders of personality, and the pilots of societies in their movement toward half-unconscious goals. I do but mention again, that the Pueblos in their complexities appear to be integrated through their symbol systems; and through their symbol systems, their social imperatives appear to become implanted as truly internalized conscience, and as precise and deep-dyed aesthetic instinct, within their individuals. Thus the Pueblo society renews itself forevermore in the Pueblo soul which it creates; thus whole tribes are co-sharers in beauty both stylized and passionate; and thus, within a severely compelling social order, the individual feels himself free and is free, being uncoerced, and making his choices within his own conscience and soul, there where the symbol system has implanted the tribal soul from of old. This subject, in terms of the Pueblos, and in world terms, has been profoundly pursued by Laura Thompson, who has drawn in part on the revealing study of the structure of the Hopi Indian language by B. F. Whorf.

Think of symbol systems and their weaving of pattern and color into the soul, and their forthshadowings of meanings and destinies that transcend words. The symbol system's vehicles are individual rhythm and mass rhythm, individual song and mass song, masks and costumes, beautiful, fantastic, sometimes awful. Its vehicles are hundreds of known and named plants whose properties are magical. They are the katcina images or "dolls," of which more than five hundred individual types are known to exist, and which represent the spirits of earth, of heaven, of water spring and sacred hill. They are the war gods of Zuñi, carved by special carvers from the wood of lightning-blasted pines. They are the rattlesnake, and the plumed serpent from out of the vanished Toltec age, symbol of the creator-god. They are the Hopi sand or dry paintings, done only within the sacred kiva, from whence, presumably, the Navajos learned their dry painting a third of a millennium ago. But the Navajo dry painting is always constructed from the center toward the periphery, the Hopi dry painting always from the periphery toward the center. Which single fact sums up the diffuse genius of the Navajo society, the concentrating genius of the Pueblo society; or possibly only or mainly of the Hopi society, the most unchanged representative of ancient pueblo life.

Add a multitude of other symbols—corn blossom and squash blossom, eagle and deer, rainbow and fire and storm cloud, the underworld which gave forth man and all creatures and will receive them again, and many symbols whose secret meaning is unrevealed to any white man. And conceive that all this multitude of symbolism is borne by solemn and sacred mass drama, in slow rhythms but with recurring crises, through the whole round of the year and through cycles of years. Conceive that each of the great movements or acts of these mass dramas is perpetuated through memory alone, is prepared for by fasting, continence, solitary vigil, and symbolic disciplines aimed toward intensity of realization. Conceive that whole ceremonial societies, even whole populations, participate creatively in the sacred drama which they know as the renewal of power ever renewed for thousands

of years; and the masked dancers believe the gods have entered and trans-
formed them, and all the people hear the rhythm of the feet of the gods of
the universe, moving from a huge past not gone and dead, but only with-
drawn below a threshold, on into a future which the gods claim for themselves and for the tribe with the help of the tribe's impassioned will and its
symbol-fraught rhythms.

Thus, if you have not witnessed a Pueblo sacred drama, you may build
for yourself some realization of the tremendous thing that it is. But only
through witnessing it can you discover what a masterpiece of color, form,
sound and mass rhythm and slow sequence of vast movements it is. Classic
as Shakespeare almost never is, but as the Greek tragic drama was, and the
Gregorian chant in its highest; classic, with intensity borne on rhythms
which hurry never: such are these pueblo sacred dramas, which number
many hundreds, each with its own burden of symbolism which for the
Pueblo Indian is nurture, power, future, prophecy, and token of union with
the Source of Things.

It is a somewhat incredible fashion among many anthropologists to remark
that the whole of this unified multitude of Pueblo sacred drama is nothing
more than an operation to make the corn grow, or to bring an emotion of
security to the afraid and insecure. Account for Chartres Cathedral thus,
for the *Bhagavad-Gita,* for Michelangelo, Plato, Aeschylus, for the Christ,
and for Bach's music. None can say what that Reality in the Universe is,
from whence the Pueblos' sacred dramas came and toward which they
march; and let one say that all is Freudian projection and mere imitative
magic, if he thinks that his hypothesis requires this bankruptcy of perception
of him. The experiencer knows what an experience is, and he alone; and
the Pueblo Indian experiencer of the sacred drama knows that he is raised
into vastness, made free from personal trouble, flooded with impersonal joy
and ardor, and plunged into the ever-flowing tide of the tribal and world
soul. And whatever the epistemological presumption be, it is a fact that
the sacred drama, at the core of Pueblo life, is a personality-forming, an
educative institution, possibly without rival in the world of today.

The statement which I have just now made calls for amplification. The
sacred dramas are the central, though by no means the only, educational
institution of the Pueblos. How, and to what educational end?

Ancient Greek education had this sort of philosophy:

Know the nature of things—the universe. The nature of things is multitude, but within law; it is orchestrated harmony. The nature of things created you, the man; and of you, every part of body and mind must be active, in due proportion, in an orchestrated harmony; and it must exist in public, must exist as public service.

Greek civilization, however, in its later and greatest phases, rested economically on slavery; excluded woman from most of life; pursued mercantile exploitation, colonial-type, with hardheartedness; and was not restrained from personal ambition and from pride by *reverence* for that universe which, through education, the Greek personality sought to match. Frederick W. H. Myers, a passionate classicist and a great modern psychologist, in his autobiographical fragment wrote:

> The Hellenism of my early years was an intellectual stimulus, but in no way a moral control. Entirely congenial to my temperament, it urged me onwards into intellectual freedom and emotional vividness, but exercised no check upon pride. Hellenism is the affirmation of the will to live—but with no projection of the desired life into any juster or sterner world.

Pueblo educational philosophy can be verbalized as Greek educational philosophy is verbalized above, without the change of a word. But these important differences in the social and intellectual situation exist:

Pueblo civilization does not rest on or include slavery; woman has her life role, different from man's but not inferior to man's; mercantilism does not exist; reverence for the universe—for the nature of things, and its law—restrains ambition and pride; and finally, there has been no storing away of knowledge and wisdom in books, so that the responsibility resting on the educational institution is far more compelling than it was in Greece.

Minor, though important, elements in Pueblo education are taken for granted here, and are merely mentioned. They include moral training through fable and precept from the elder to the young; learning, through example and through direct teaching, of the techniques of the hunt, of farming and animal husbandry, of the preservation and preparation of foods; learning of the crafts, from weaving and pottery and mural painting and costume making to house building and church and town building; and learning the uncompensated duties of public work and public office. Not one of these minor phases of education is wholly apart from the major phase; the major phase motivates and conditions them all, within that free-moving integration which distinguishes Pueblo life. Now, to the major phase.

The Pueblos

I here draw upon the results of a Research into Indian Education which was launched as a cooperative project by the United States Indian Service in 1941, which utilized many scientific specializations, and whose published results are being issued in successive volumes now. A number of Indian tribes of contrasting cultures and situations were studied profoundly, and one of these was the Hopi tribe. I quote from a volume, as yet unpublished, which extends the findings of *The Hopi Way,* published in 1944. The published volume was written by Laura Thompson, anthropologist, and Alice Joseph, physician and psychiatrist. The manuscript here quoted is by Laura Thompson.

We have noted the vital role played by the Hopi ceremonial organization and ceremonial cycle in the development and maintenance of Hopi social and personality health and balance. . . .

Hopi ceremonies form a logical complex which symbolizes the traditional Hopi world view. They depict a series of related mythical episodes, the annual rendition of which is believed necessary for the harmonious operation of the universe. Indeed, if man does not carry out his ceremonial obligations faithfully, and even with supreme effort of his will, the functioning of the cosmic web of life uniting nature and man will be impaired. The sun may fail to turn back from his winter "house," rain may not fall, and plants, animals, and human beings may not bear fruit.

To present Hopi ritual as a means designed solely to bring rain (as is usually done, even by scientists) is to throw out of focus the whole picture of Hopi religion, and to misrepresent the basic orientation of Hopi culture and personality.

The universal character of Hopi ritual is shown, for example, in the Winter Solstice ceremony which inaugurates the annual cycle. Dramatic rites, designed to turn the Sun back northward from his winter "house," give the ceremony a cosmic cast. But also, as part of the ceremony, prayer sticks are made for practically every order of natural phenomena important to Hopi life. They are made for specific human beings and ancestors, for non-human partners, for useful animals and plants, for dwelling houses, fields, shrines, growing crops, and even for all mankind. Thus, while the Winter Solstice ceremony emphasizes the yearly cycle of the Sun and its significance in the universal scheme, it also expresses the whole Hopi world view with its stress on reciprocal interdependence, the emergence of the tribe from the Underworld and its migration to its present location, as well as the cosmic life process. It is clear that the Winter Solstice ceremony is many-sided in its underlying significance. A brief survey of the other major Hopi ceremonies discloses that each may likewise be interpreted at several levels. Individually and as a cycle, they comprise a logical complex which expresses the traditional Hopi world view. The whole cycle, as well as each single ceremony, is a subtly orchestrated unit combining many art media—rhythmic movement, singing, drumming, impersonation, painting—to express in a highly stylized manner one ever-recurring theme—namely, the Hopi world view.

Indians of the Southwest

When we study the ceremonial complex in its setting, we find that what may appear to us on the surface to be a strange conglomeration of colorful dances and weird music, actually expresses a logical implicit philosophy which unifies and gives meaning to Hopi culture and behavior. An inside view reveals that Hopi ritual articulates an implicit system of concepts, values and attitudes which are highly integrated both from the viewpoint of logic and from the viewpoint of art.

Although clothed in unfamiliar raiment, the message is simple and its key ideas are reiterated again and again. Briefly they are: the unity and rhythm of nature; the correlative interdependence of nature and man; natural law as the basis for human law; the pervading power of prayer, ritual, art, and concentration on the "good"; the folly of quarrelsomeness, pride, and non-cooperation; freedom through education and self-discipline. Order and rhythm are in the nature of things. It behooves man to study them and to bring his life and his society into harmony with them. Only so may he be free. . . .

The Law (the Hopi believe) requires that, to be effective, man must participate not merely by performing certain rites at prescribed intervals in certain ways; but he must also participate with his emotions and thoughts, by prayer and willing. . . .

Hopi traditional philosophy, therefore, ascribes to man a purposive, creative role in the universe—a role which centers in the development of his will. The universe is not conceived as a sort of machine at the mercy of mechanical law. Nor is it viewed as a sum total of hostile, competitive forces struggling for existence. It is by nature a harmonious, integrated system operating rhythmically according to the principles of immanent justice, and in it the key rôle is played by man's will.

I pause from quotation to answer an expostulation which may arise in your mind, the Reader's. "Surely," you may exclaim, "it is a remarkable aesthetic-religious construction, this Hopi belief and its ritual embodiment. And well it may be an energy-generating and disciplinary force in the individual Hopi's life, and a conserver and regenerator of Hopi society. A marvelous human construction, but surely it must go down the wind of time, for it is prescientific or antiscientific." Is there an answer?

We of the Occidental world tried for hundreds of years to believe that God as a moving principle in the world (as anything more than an ideal in the human heart) was pre- and anti-scientific. We tried to believe that free choice and free will in man—even the minutest atom of them—were useful illusions, and in a deterministic universe could not be more. How patiently and resourcefully we tried, for a hundred years, to conceive organic life as being chemistry alone, and to divest the life process of creativity and directiveness. Is it only the stubborn animism and wishfulness of the human soul that is pushing informed and sophisticated minds away from the bravely maintained positivistic world view? Or is it the mounting accumulation of facts on many lines?

66

The Pueblos

Enough to suggest: If the Pueblo creed is dated and doomed by the regnancy of deterministic science, then the Christian and Buddhist creeds no less are dated and doomed, and the belief in the power of ideals to move men or events. Let us not, to the few and weak, apply negations which we do not apply to the many and strong. If Pueblo creed is dated fantasy, then most of the far, world-moving human hope is dated fantasy too.

I resume the quotation. To what human fruitage—what practiced code of morals and manners—does the Hopi philosophy and its symbolic expression in sacred drama lead?

The Hopi's personal ideal is to live, to the utmost of one's powers, for society (as envisaged in Hopi terms)—i.e., to live for the pueblo unit. He who approaches most nearly the ideal is the individual who is most completely self-realized and also socialized, in Hopi terms.

The Hopi have set up a definite standard for personal conduct, and this standard is expressed in the vernacular by the word *hopi*. Whereas much of Hopi ideology is expressed only by implication, Hopi tradition is explicit on this point.

The term *hopi* is usually translated as "peaceful, good, happy." But it actually connotes all those attributes that to the Hopi make up the balanced, Law-fulfilling whole of mind and body which is man as he should be. The good (*hopi*) person is:

1. *Strong* (in the Hopi sense, i.e., he is both morally and physically strong);
2. *Poised* (in the Hopi sense, i.e., he is balanced, free of anxiety, tranquil, "quiet of heart," concentrated on "good" thoughts);
3. *Law-abiding* (i.e., responsible, actively cooperative, kind, and unselfish);
4. *Peaceful* (i.e., non-aggressive, non-quarrelsome, modest);
5. *Protective* (i.e., fertility-promoting and life-preserving, rather than injurious or destructive to life in any of its manifestations, including human beings, animals, and plants);
6. *Free from illness.*

One further quotation, because it goes to the heart of Pueblo society.

Let us compare the Hopi precept with the Golden Rule: "Do unto others as you would they should do unto you." The Hopi code, reduced to a simple maxim, might read: "Cultivate the Hopi Way, and you and the whole people will have peace, prosperity, and happiness." Both teachings emphasize the development of an ideal norm of conduct within the individual. But the Christian precept defines the ideal pattern of behavior for the individual in terms of his dealings with other individuals, on the assumption that altruistic inter-personal relations will automatically solve the problems of group living. The Hopi rule stresses the view that the individual is one of the units within a complex and patterned social whole, and that the whole will function harmoniously only through his assumption of complete personal responsibility as a member of society, and not simply as an individual. The Hopi rule differs from the Golden Rule mainly in its emphasis on the social ideal toward which the individual ideal is pointed. For the orthodox Hopi, ethics and politics are one.

A number of pages back, a statement is made and a question asked. "Pueblo policy became the fine flower of the realized Laws of the Indies. Over the long span, it can be said that Spain allowed the Pueblo civilizations to live into our own day. Will we allow them to live into a day beyond our own?"

There are aspects of Pueblo life other than, and complementary to, those already set down, and subsequent pages will allude to them. But here is the place to expand the paragraph quoted above.

The Indian record of Spain, which is the longest in years of all modern colonial records, is a book of stupendous drama—in the main, tragic drama of darkest hue. In one aspect, it is a drama within the soul of a nation and race, Spain herself. It commenced as a thunderstorm of ruin, whose rain-drops were the blood of millions of Indians and the pulverized wreckage of many great Indian cultures and societies. Then, from within Spain's own soul, mighty efforts at redemption took their rise. The drama complicated itself. Wise, far-seeing practical statesmanship, great humanitarianism, great spiritual affirmations, were confronted by the rapacity of church, state, *conquistadores* and colonists, by the religious fanaticism and the active cruelty of the age, by the Byzantine autocracy and bureaucracy of the Span-ish administrative machine; and at the heart of the drama, by gigantic un-wisdom in the brains of the very men whose intentions were noblest. Not here can that tale be told, but something must be told of the Dominican friar Bartolomé de Las Casas, and what his life's work led to, because they connect with the Pueblos of yesterday, today, and tomorrow.

Las Casas was born at Seville in 1474. He became the first Christian priest ordained in the New World. Himself an owner of Indian slaves and holder of an *encomienda* (a grant of land with Indians attached as serfs), he under-went, when nearing middle age, a spiritual revolution, a true "second birth," through the influence of certain Dominican monks.

His conversion was to the goodness, beauty, and spiritual potency of the Indians, and to the principle of unlimited freedom of conscience for Indians. He became the greatest of the advocates the Indian has ever known, and one of the greatest of the apostles of human liberty. He preached and wrote, and lobbied at the Spanish court, and went among the Indians; in Guatemala, practically singlehanded, he converted a warlike nation of Indians to Christianity through love and reason alone. He withheld no denunciation of wrongdoers toward Indians, let the lightning strike where it might; his writings became the property of all Europe, and were used as a Protestant weapon against the Catholic Church (for the Spanish king was head of the Church itself in all save doctrinal matters, in Spain and the New World, by papal grant). Las Casas' own monastic order, the Dominican, had brought into being the Inquisition, whose balefires were burning terribly in Spain in Las Casas' day; yet never did Inquisition, or Crown, or Papacy move to silence Las Casas or to discipline him. His enormous activity continued until his death in his ninety-second year.

History has recorded Las Casas' activities and deeds, but has given slight attention to his philosophy or inspiration. His inspiration came through direct vision; his philosophy was grounded in Saint Augustine. It aggrandized the human will, and insisted that the will was free; through the human will, God's will and love flowed into men and man; and the freedom must be an utterly unconditioned freedom. Las Casas projected an utopia of the New World, and vainly urged it on the Spanish crown. Only men of God should be allowed to enter the New World at all; and these men should be "screened" through a searching personnel work. They must be men believing in the Indians and believing in freedom and in the City of God which only spiritually free men could build within human society. In retrospect, and in the light of the events which his inspiration led to, we see today that Las Casas' social philosophy was an incomplete one. He perceived with burningness the individual, and the "abysmal deeps of personality." He perceived the absolutely momentous principle of individual liberty. He did not perceive *society*, that "congregation of the lone" as it may appear within the introspective mind, that intangible but unerring and age-outlasting feeder, shaper and sustainer of the soul, as modern social anthropology knows it to be.

From Las Casas there flowed, through centuries, in North and South America, those famous labors of the monastic orders among Indians which gave us in the United States the California Indian missions. The supreme achievement was in Paraguay—an area much larger than the present Paraguay. There, the Jesuits brought into being a true utopia, a theocratic communism whose membership numbered up to one hundred and fifty thousands, and who never were served or ruled by as many as a hundred white men at one time. There, all of European technology functioned in communities which knew no want, no fear, and no coercion; the arts flowered miraculously, and life moved onward as a happy river of shining moods.

But in Paraguay, as in California, and almost certainly everywhere except in one region soon to be identified, these utopias took no account of, or were actively negative toward, the *native societies* of the Indians who were their population. Whole-cloth, new, substitute societies were decreed and were accomplished. The result ultimately was fatal to the Indians and to the noble hopes of the monastic orders. In California, for example, the Mission Indians became extinct in the process of becoming missionized, and all but a handful of the remnant were dead within a few years after the secularizing of the missions by Mexico in 1825. In Paraguay, after the expulsion of the Jesuits by Spain in the 1760's, the most beautiful *practical* utopia which the world has known (and it lasted 150 years) dissolved into the wilderness and the grave.

Let us return, now, to the New Mexico Pueblos. Las Casas wrote the New Laws of the Indies in 1542. He saw them all canceled out before ten years had gone by; but as the decades rolled on, the New Laws became re-enacted and elaborated and also they became implemented. In 1680, the Spaniards were driven from New Granada (New Mexico) through the united revolt of all the Pueblos, including the Hopi Pueblos. In 1688, Spain came back. The years since 1540, when Coronado had entered New Granada, had established as a stark fact that the Pueblo societies could not be broken down by any means short of killing all the Indians. And Spain absolutely required the Pueblos; they were the barrier against the wild tribes, Apaches, Comanches, Cheyennes, Navajos. They were also the grainery on which local colonization depended. The Pueblos' stern action of 1680 clinched the case; and after the reconquest, Spain put the Laws of the Indies into full force and effect, with that all-crucial factor added, which Las Casas and those who came after him had not understood. That is, Spain acknowledged the domestic autonomy of the Pueblos, accepted their immemorial societies, incorporated these societies within the Spanish Empire. At Spain's instance, the Pueblos had established the office of secular governor of the pueblo: he mediated with the outer world as the instrument of the traditional social order and of the real, covert Pueblo government, and he effectively shielded the Pueblos' internal life—the Pueblos' universe—from the whole white world, state, church and army alike.

This course of events explains why Spain allowed the ancient Pueblos to

The Pueblos

live on, slowly equating themselves with the white world while keeping, even deepening, their inner, plastic endowment and their complex genius born in other ages than ours. It explains why these mountain heights of the sunken social continent still lift their pinnacles and domes in living air.

Thus we are brought to the question filled with fate: Will we, the United States, like Spain, allow the Pueblos to live on, even into a day beyond our own?

There is no open-and-shut answer. If every existent fact, factor and trend were scientifically known, still neither Yes nor No could be pronounced with certainty. The answer rests in the supply or non-supply of future creative effort by the Pueblos themselves and their white friends. I shall try to state some of the factors in the problem.

The Pueblos took their forms and developed them through fifteen hundred years or longer, amid physical hardship and almost incessant danger— warfare and drought, and then white encroachment. The hardship and danger were not mere liabilities, since the Pueblos met them creatively through institutions and value systems which transmuted danger and hardship into character, into social form and individual and social strength, and into the mystic splendors which flash from out of the Pueblo soul.

Since (after the white man came) direct assault against the Pueblo life system (in the early Spanish years, and all the American years until the late 1920's) could not kill or even weaken the life system, this direct assault served as warfare had done in prehistory: it strengthened the Pueblos. Even the remorseless land encroachment by whites, which went ahead from the end of the Spanish dominion to the year 1922, and which forced chronic famine on many of the Pueblos, was unavailing to break their life system or to weaken it. In 1922, Secretary Albert B. Fall, of the Interior Department, and his Indian Bureau, launched an all-out, final attack against the Pueblos, designed to strip them of their land base and smash their institutions and religious cultures at the same time. I had the good fortune to be in contact with each of the twenty-one New Mexico pueblos, through 1922 and the eight crisis years following. The contact was intimate. I could witness how the joy of battle burned at the deep levels of Pueblo life, threshold below threshold, door beyond door; and the thrillingly competent thinking that went on there, in wise old men and wise young men too. The city-states formed their Union of All the Pueblos again; it had been latent since 1680. They maintained stability and collective volition through the legislative and court battles which lasted, actually, eleven years. They took their case to the American people from coast to coast, and became the spear-head of all the Indian peoples in that struggle which, in 1933, overturned the old Indian Bureau and reversed the government's policy of liquidat-ing the Indians. Their inner deeps of life were coping with the world in new ways. The Pueblo self-creation, and its adjustment and renewal of the ancient life system, were vividly evident through those years of crisis— years of resistance against assault, which moved into years of victorious advance.

In the years following 1935, two of the pueblos faced a crisis due to soil erosion—the same crisis with which the Navajos have been struggling since 1933. Acoma, for example, was running 33,000 sheep units on a wrecked range whose carrying capacity was only 8,500 sheep units. All the tech-nological facts were assembled. The Acomas were decisively told that no compulsion would be used by the government on them. In community meetings lasting many weeks, all the data and every consideration was laid before Acoma's leadership and rank and file alike. The painful, almost im-possibly difficult adjustments were left to Acoma to bring about in its own way and in genuine freedom. Acoma fully and brilliantly met the test, made the sacrifices, mastered the new soil techniques and upbreeding and market-ing techniques, and saved and regenerated its range. Its institutional forces and inner unity were strengthened and expanded through the action which coped with the world. The identical record could be given for Laguna pueblo, Acoma's near neighbor.

So far, the answer to our question—Shall the Pueblos survive, in the ways of their ancient genius?—appears as an optimistic one. Assault from with-out, and the arrival of great, obvious crises which have to be met by drawing on all the inner powers, nearly always has strengthened the Pueblos, not weakened, denatured or effaced them. I write "nearly always" because there has been one exception, that of the Hopi Third Mesa, which will be men-tioned below. The exception does not alter the rule.

And the future holds many and sure challenges, comparable to those that have gone before, and ample to strike every chord of deep will in Pueblo life. New legislative drives to strip the Pueblos of their lands are already assured. The livestock and wool-growers associations, implacably predatory against conservation and against Indian grazing rights, are even now pre-paring heavier onsets. The Pueblos along the Rio Grande confront, along

The Pueblos

with all the other populations, the certainty of extinction in times not far ahead, unless the accelerated erosion of the Rio Grande watershed in its entirety can be stopped. New drives within Congress to break down every safeguard of the Indians' landholdings will be in full swing before this book is published. Each and all of these perils and crises will tend to strengthen internally the Pueblos' life, *other things being equal*.

But other things are not equal; and here we come to the less optimistic part of the picture.

First to note, is the increase of Pueblo population. It goes ahead at nearly two per cent a year. The Pueblos, with the solitary exception of Sandia, near Albuquerque, are outgrowing their land bases. They have not the capital or the available credit for large purchases of new land. Sooner with some of the Pueblos, later with others, emigration will be necessary. By itself, this fact is not necessarily fatal or even damaging to the Pueblo life system. But it is not a fact by itself.

The war and war services took most of the young men out of the Pueblos, for terms up to six years. Ceremonial life is at the core of the Pueblo institution and personality. It was stopped for a number of years in the case of these young men, and all the Pueblo rhythms were broken in their lives. They received a heavy dose of American material "standard of living" values; they were pushed almost irresistibly toward externalism of life. The long-term consequences cannot yet be foretold. By itself, the interruption and temporary reorientation need not be fatal or even damaging to the Pueblo institution; but again, it is not a factor by itself.

In self-defense, the Pueblos will be compelled to claim the political franchise and to use it. They have it now. If New Mexico's Indians as voters stand together, they will become the balance-of-power group in that state. In the Pueblo societies, public service is given without pay, and corruption is nearly if not totally unknown; and public service is all within the orbit of the Pueblos' central institution—its symbol-bearing religion. In the white world, public service is done for pay, corruption is rather usual, and cynicism and selfishness are generally taken for granted. The image of the Pueblos as arenas of New Mexico politics gives fear to many of the wise old leaders. Once more, this prospect by itself is not necessarily fatal.

The truly deadly peril which the Pueblos face is not any one or all together of those limned above, except as they are elements in a wider condition. That condition is, simply, the acutely multiplied contacts of the Pueblo young people with the white world—the white middle-class world, to which the great realities of Pueblo life are not realities at all, not even existences at all. We all know this white world: its concentration on externals, on "upward mobility," on conveniences and on unmeaningful sensation and material security: a world of wholesome human nature and of social drift, and of no long dwelling with any deep ideas. This world takes for granted its own finality and omnipotence; and increased contact with it and immersion in it must of necessity, on the average, weaken the young Indian's belief in his Pueblo and diminish his sensitiveness toward its ancient summons, called from the housetops at twilight and dawn. And the major programs of Indian Service itself, the aesthetic and intellectual taste of Indian Service, and not least, its teaching personnel, are of this white middle-class world, in the main; the Indians on school and agency staffs usually are recruits from Oklahoma, the Lake States, the Plains and the West Coast, themselves zealously acculturated into white middle-class values and preconceptions.

The Pueblos, in all their ages, have not confronted a peril like this one before. It is an assault against their power to keep their own soul alive, in the form of a casual, good-natured assault by the white world against the dawning souls of their young people. It is an all-pervading, undramatic, unconcentrated, ubiquitous peril. If the Pueblos prove able to surmount it, they will have gained the most conclusive of all their victories over time and change. I believe that with the help of an Indian Service changed in ways difficult but not impossible, they *could* surmount this, their final peril.

Very much in brief, this is what I mean by a changed Indian Service, difficult but not impossible. It would be a service specialized to the Pueblos' problem, just as there should be a service specialized to the Navajos' problem, and the Sioux', the Papagos' and the Eskimos' problems. A true "career service," of men and women sought out and enlisted because they would have the endowment of devotion, attitudes and personality structure to fit them to understand both the Pueblos and the wider world. These men and women would then be trained and retrained through that method of democratic group self-education known as action research.

They would work as advisers to the Pueblos, seeking to help the Pueblos to equip their own young people for every Pueblo task, including all of the government's tasks of Pueblo service.

They would presume—accurately—a high, not low, intelligence quotient in the Pueblos, a large, not small, capacity for discriminative and integrative thinking and for social invention, and a great, not petty, destiny as members of mankind.

They would change, gradually and experimentally but radically, the emphases in the government's Pueblo schools: allowing the unexampled aesthetic richness and potency of the Pueblo nature to come into play; building in the young people an awareness of Pueblo values in terms of the whole world's desperate need, and of world time beyond the present extremely unrepresentative and fast-fading hour.

They would help the Pueblo leaders to see the Pueblo in terms of the great world, and world need in terms of pueblo creative power.

Within this sort of help from a possible Indian Service, I deeply believe that the Pueblos could and would surmount the most fateful danger and crisis of their thousands of years. Without this sort of help, the Pueblos, not as mere aggregations of human beings, but as citadels of a great, ancient and timeless spirit, may die.

Ever since 1933, the basic policies of Indian Service have pointed toward this kind of change in the government's working method with Indians. The Indian Reorganization Act of 1934 made these policies the basic Indian law of the United States; it is the basic law now. In my own twelve years as Indian Commissioner, I was not able decisively to bring about the changed orientation and structure in day-to-day Indian Service which is outlined so briefly above; and I do not see much progress toward the change now, nor is the general political climate favorable to it. But it remains the hope of the Pueblos, and of all the other tribes and groups of tribes whose creative heritage has not yet died, or whose ecological situation is unique; and of these there are many. And it remains the opportunity of the United States to build a trail far out into that obscure yet world-critical area known as the area of the minorities and dependent peoples. This text is no place for a fuller discussion of the need and possibility.

About the long future of the Pueblos, then, as of the Navajos, we cannot yet know. It depends on creative actions, their own and ours, which may or may not be supplied.

Chapter 7

THE APACHES

THE whole world knows something of the Apache Indians—inveterate, predatory warriors. Geronimo! The name rings with terror and with wonder yet. With fighters numbering hardly a hundred, and encumbered with all the women and children, the sick and aged of the band, he fought the United States army through years. Masters of strategy and tactics and of "intelligence," these Apaches were the incomparable guerrilla fighters of all time.

Geronimo surrendered to General Nelson A. Miles in 1886. Half of his band had perished in the last of his wars, and the Apaches were to fight no more until the world wars should come. Geronimo and his band were exiled to Florida, then to Alabama, then to Oklahoma; finally they were settled in the Mescalero Apache reservation, in south-central New Mexico. A spacious and beautiful place it is. In midsummer one climbs toward its magic mountain's crest along slopes shoulder deep in flowers, and to the west he sees the world of the white sands with its vast, gleaming, moveless waves.

Their war way ended, the Apaches became known to reporters on Indian life as peoples sunken in melancholy, existing in gray squalor at the expense of the government, idle prisoners in concentration camps under a sometimes kindly despotism; and in northern New Mexico, the Jicarilla Apaches ebbed toward extinction; the ebb was not reversed until twenty years ago.

But the Apaches' long year was not ended. They are Athapascan peoples, as are the Navajos, and their adaptive and assimilative power and resiliency are very great. These Athapascans are among the latest comers to the Western Hemisphere from Asia; and when reading of the almost fabulous social vitality of some of the aboriginal Mongoloid groups within the Soviet sphere, one is reminded of the Apaches. Commencing about ten years ago, those Apache groups whom Ira Moskowitz pictures here (the Mescaleros and Jicarillas) have emerged as true achievers on lines economic and political. Their self-governing institutions have become models of economy,

The Apaches

efficiency and probity; they have proved to be credit risks actually one hundred per cent reliable; they have shown that they can do long-range social and economic planning and can triumphantly pursue their plans; and the Jicarillas have built themselves a cooperative commonwealth of entirely modern forms, possibly the most complete to be found in the Western Hemisphere. This achievement will be told later in this chapter.

White minds' eyes find it not easy to see the Apaches as they really, inwardly are. Paradoxes abound. Why is it that the most warlike of tribes (and the men were the warriors) organizes its most important religious, aesthetic and social event around its girls just entering on puberty? Why is it that peace in the heart is made the central aim of the principal ceremony of peoples who lived by and for war? How is it that groups of humans who seem content to live, in the domestic way, rather uncouthly and untidily, with little apparent instinct for organization, can on the one hand develop and operate the precise, many-sided cooperative institution of Jicarilla, while on the other hand they carry in memory cycle upon cycle of anciently beautiful poems, recited for the whole community to enjoy and be molded by?

Here is one of these poems.* It is the fifty-third song in one of the adolescent ceremonies for girls, at Mescalero. The translation is by P. E. Goddard in his *Gotal: a Mescalero Apache Ceremony*. The ritual as a whole dramatizes the creation of nature and its perennial renewals; the Masked Dancers are there, representing the Gods of the Sacred Mountains, but known to uninitiated whites as Devil Dancers. As generally with Indian ceremonials, this one seeks joyful union of all the participants with the Source of Things.

The black turkey gobbler, under the east, the middle of his tail; toward us it is about
    to dawn.
The black turkey gobbler, the tips of his beautiful tail; above us the dawn whitens.
The black turkey gobbler, the tips of his beautiful tail; above us the dawn becomes
    yellow.
The sunbeams stream forward, dawn boys, with shimmering shoes of leather.
On top of the sunbeams that stream toward us they are dancing.
At the east the rainbow moves forward, dawn maidens, with shimmering shoes and
    shirts of yellow, stream over us.
Beautiful over us it is dawning.

Above us among the mountains the herbs are becoming green.
Above us on the tops of the mountains the herbs are becoming yellow.

* *The Black Turkey Gobbler Chant,* published by permission of the Executors of the Estate of Pliny E. Goddard.

Indians of the Southwest

Above us among the mountains, with shoes of yellow I go around the fruits and the
  herbs that shimmer.
Above us among the mountains, the shimmering fruits with shoes and shirts of yellow
  are bent toward him (the Sun).
On the beautiful mountains above, it is daylight.

Here is another of the countless poems or chants of the Apaches. It tells
how their gods appear to them, and how the relationship between the gods
and man is a loving one, and how the need flows two ways—not only from
man to the gods, but from the gods to man. The translator is Harry Hoijer,
in *Chiricahua and Mescalero Apache Texts.**

Big Blue Mountain Spirit,
The home made of blue clouds,
The cross made of the blue mirage,
There, you have begun to live,
There, is the life of goodness,
I am grateful for that made of goodness there.

Big Yellow Mountain Spirit in the south,
Your spiritually hale body is made of yellow clouds;
Leader the Mountain Spirits, holy Mountain Spirit,
You live by means of the good of this life.

Big White Mountain Spirit in the west,
Your spiritually hale body is made of the white mirage;
Holy Mountain Spirit, leader of the Mountain Spirits,
I am happy over your words,
You are happy over my words.

Big Black Mountain Spirit in the north,
Your spiritually hale body is made of black clouds;
In that way, Big Black Mountain Spirit,
Holy Mountain Spirit, leader of the Mountain Spirits,
I am happy over your words,
You are happy over my words,
Now it is good.

In Apache religion and cosmology, the "nebulous and remote Supreme
Being" (Opler), who is called Life Giver, mediates through gods who are
nearer to earth and man. One of Morris Opler's informants explained:
  "When a person has a special ceremony, from Lightning, for instance, he

* Published by permission of the University of Chicago Press.

will pray directly to Lightning and will not call on Life Giver. But many feel that Life Giver is answering through this other source."

Less remote, and very important as a symbol, is White Painted Woman, who is Mother Earth. And Child of the Water is a god of the middle distance. At a time near the beginning of things, "when the lightning flashed four times and acted as a man to beget Child of the Water," White Painted Woman conceived and bore Child of the Water, a deified culture hero analogous to Quetzalcoatl, the Toltec and Aztec culture hero and maker of the Mexican golden age which would yet return.

Nearer to man in the present are the Mountain Spirits or Mountain Gods, addressed in the poem last quoted above. Their home is the interior of the Sacred Mountains, but these imagined sacred caverns "measureless to man" symbolize even the universe; all imagery of earth and sky is used in addressing the Mountain Gods.

In healing ceremonies and in the warding off of epidemics, as well as in the girls' puberty rites, the Mountain Gods are represented by the Masked Dancers; and the Masked Dancers, whose role, in the ceremonies to ward off epidemics, is a momentous and solemn one, at the girls' puberty ceremony may be rather the spreaders of gaiety. There is laughter in the world, not only in the heart of man, the Apaches know; Nietzsche's "Dancing Star" could be their image of God and the gods; and the sacred role includes the role of the clown, as we have noted in the case of the Pueblos too.

A word, here, on the translations of Apache poetry, as of most other poetry of the Indians.

The Apache poem is a song, and the song is merely one of the threads woven into a religious-philosophical-aesthetic fabric. The thread within the fabric and its pattern is something quite other than the thread when taken out from the fabric. The faithfully translated words of an Apache poem are somewhat like the thread after being unraveled from the fabric.

The same can be remarked of the other threads—the dance, the drumming and rattling, the costume, the music of the voice in chant, the many symbolical actions, and the long rhythms which move across the whole of the synthesis as the ritual drama proceeds through four nights and days.

This remark is very true in the cases where the words of the poem are lifted out from the context of the more solemn, intense movements of the ritual drama, but it is true even of song-poems belonging to the lighter moments. I quote Morris Opler, in *An Apache Life-Way:*

Indians of the Southwest

The few words of an Apache social dance song are rich in implication. Once an old man dismissed American songs with a contemptuous "There isn't much singing to them; it's all words!" Doubtless he was thinking of the more subtle technique of his people, by which, with a few well-chosen words and a wealth of inner meaning, a dozen youths can be made to hang their heads.

The Indian poem is not words alone, but is ritual drama as one indivisible production or event. Let that whole production or event be reduced to statement, with the meanings of the symbols explained; then, if one gives himself with sustained imagination to the whole of it, he can partly sound the deeps of the verbalized parts of the songs. Then let one be present at the ritual drama, not merely for an hour but for its whole duration, there by night and day in the passionately beautiful land, and let him open his soul to the contagion of the Indians' emotion: now at last he will experience the greatness of the orchestrated art of these prayer-dramas, art very ancient, perhaps ten thousand years ancient, yet wholly living now.

And yet, there is another reservation to make. The prayer-dramas do not exist merely by themselves; in nearly their whole reference, they have a dual orientation—toward the universe, the gods, and the deeps of the human consciousness, and toward the community in all its workaday aspects. They are the tribe's main educational and personality-forming institution; its main public health and clinical institution; and one of its main institutions for the establishment and strengthening of human relationships. Thus, in the one orientation they are cosmical in their intent and meaning, while in the other orientation they are domestic, civic, sociological. Romantically mystical, and realistically practical within the world which their knowledge reaches: thus are the prayer-dramas, and thus are the Apache peoples. Thus was very ancient man; the Apaches until yesterday were near indeed to ancient man. What a profound *sanity* have these little groups of Indians, the sanity and balanced many-sidedness of many of the societies of ancient man. The loss of that profound sanity from our cosmopolitan world in its individualism and rushes of blind power is the loss of a golden age which veritably existed in aeons of our human time; there are human groups, where still moves on the sanity of that golden age. Is the future world denied that sort of golden age forever? Certainly not, since the human power has not vanished, but is only functionally deranged. Certainly not, since the universe which made us has not changed. And since new, young lives will forever be taking their departure from the biological germ plasm which has not changed; and since

The Apaches

science will focus itself at the ecological-social level where all of destiny abides, and then mankind will find the way once more. Meanwhile, precious indeed are these little societies which demonstrate, in our epoch cynical and desperate, that the flight of dream and the most practical of human communities are not meant to be aliens and alternatives or opposites, but to be mutually supporting, interpenetrating, inseparable, in a life hygienic and sane.

This interplay of the domestic and everyday with the cosmical is illustrated in the girls' puberty ceremony, the Apaches' most momentous ritual. Her family feels joy as the time for her first menstrual flow draws near. Preparations for the ceremony begin a year in advance. These preparations are so extensive as to exceed the resources of the family, and individuals outside the kinship group lend their aid. Garments for the girl are ceremonially made from doeskin or buckskin. "The garments are decorated with designs symbolic of the forces which will be supplicated on behalf of the girl. The morning star and the crescent moon may be represented, as may a stepped design representing the dwelling. Circles indicate the sun, and fringes streaming from their centers, the sunbeams. Connected arcs stand for the rainbow. Before the dress is finished, all parts have to be colored yellow, the hue of pollen. Yellow ocher may be rubbed on, or the buckskin may be dyed in a liquid prepared from algerta roots. The dress must be blessed as well as beautifully finished. 'The singer is usually an old woman,' an informant stated. 'She sometimes sings over the garments for two months.' "*

A priest and a priestess (called "singer" and "attendant") are besought to conduct the ceremony. There is, of course, no priestly class; any man may become a diagnosing and healing shaman or a singer, any woman an attendant. Each must know much, and be pure of heart and possessed with reverence. For the puberty rite, the singer and attendant are chosen with care; because not merely is the rite a momentous one, but a lifelong relationship is formed between the girl and the priest and priestess. They become "father" and "mother" to her, and gifts, services and affection are exchanged throughout life.

At the ceremony, which lasts four days, the girl *becomes* White Painted Woman, Mother Earth. The ceremony symbolically reproduces earth creation, man creation, and the history of earth and man, and it carries the girl symbolically through all the stages of her future life, into happy old age.

* *An Apache Life-Way*, by Morris Opler.

81

Indians of the Southwest

The girl, herself, is not a spectator or one being passively prayed over, but is an active participant in the ritual.

The entire tribe is invited to the ceremony and to its feasts. The gradual, exquisite solemnities of the creation story and the life prophecy are recessed for a while, each day; the Masked Dancers bring noise and merrymaking as well as awe, and all the people join in round dances, in the singing of songs of love, and in the feast.

The details of the ceremony would require a hundred pages to tell. Their spirit is intimated in the two songs which have been quoted. The effect upon the girl is necessarily profound, and wholly benign. Her family, and all the people, through a rite filled with mystery and beauty, are helping her to become one worthy to carry on the tradition and blood of her race; she is being made, and is making herself from within, with the help of the gods, into the image of the Mother Earth.

And as for the use of the ceremony in the expanding and strengthening of human relations: An Apache informant is speaking to Opler.

"If you choose one of these men (to be singer) you are brother to him all of your life, even if you are not related to him. You call him friend, but you think just as much of him as you do of your brother. He thinks of your children as his children. After the ceremony is over, you give each other some valuable things—saddles, horses, anything that is worth something. When a man is poor, he gives what he can; it doesn't matter. They might come out equal in giving things to each other." These words would apply to the priestess (attendant) equally.

Now, for a variety of brief items, to expand the picture of Apache life.

The play life of the children, boys and girls alike and together, is extraordinarily resourceful and rich. The children organize expeditions to hunt for rare wild plants and flowers. They chase butterflies, always releasing them unhurt; they even chase large birds, and run them down in wet weather. They fabricate all kinds of toys and tools. They imitate the grown-up activities; boys and girls under six years mimic marriage, and set up homemaking together, but without any sexual involvement. Freedom, and a tenderness on the part of adults which is undemonstrative except at crises of emotion, is the all but universal experience of the children.

At six to eight years, the boys enter upon their disciplines, largely self-imposed, toward physical hardihood, mastery of the wild, mastery of weapons, and horsemanship.

The Apaches

Training is constant, from parents and other elders to the young. The training is in manners and morals, in the technologies of the tribe, in the traditions and the meanings of the symbols. And the child, girl or boy, is helped to share in all the adult preoccupations, joys and fears.

In warfare, the Apaches took no male prisoners. They allowed the women and girl children to flee, and killed the adult males; the Mexican male prisoners were delivered to the women to be killed. But the boys of the enemy were captured, and became sons of their captor, and entered fully into the tribe. Sometimes, women did not flee but were captured. They were never violated, and were not enslaved, and when taken to the Apache homeland they must be won through love. This, even in the case of Mexican women, though the Apaches assert that their own women when captured were always raped by the Mexicans.

Witchcraft is rather important among the Apaches. Contests between the witches' power and the shamans' power go forward all the time. Sometimes witches are murdered or executed; but not among the Apaches or any other Indians is there record of such institutionalized hysteria of witch-hunting and witch-torture and burning as were known in England and early New England.

Among the Apaches, sexual obscenity is not unknown but is scornfully resisted. Homosexuality is tabu and is extremely rare. Masturbation is asserted to be nonexistent, and Opler credits the assertion.

The traditional Apache dwelling is built by the women. It is a circular, dome-shaped brush structure, waterproofed with hide laid over the outer thatching. There is a central fireplace, and a venthole above it. Unlike the Navajo hogan, which always faces east, the Apache wickiup may face in any direction. The dwelling and its furnishings all indicate a life dependent on the chase and on wild flora, a life which moved seasonally from place to place.

All Apache bands knew and were hospitable toward one another, but the political unit was the band, not the tribe. Band leadership was democratic, based on wisdom, natural magnetism and leadership power, and willingness to carry the load. Leadership was hereditary only in that a father who qualified as a leader was expected to rear a son who would be his equal in virtue. Leaders were not chosen by an electoral process, nor was talent sought out when young and systematically trained toward leadership, as in the Pueblos; rather, leadership appears to have grown into being through the general acceptance by the people that a man was intellectually and morally worthy.

Particular items like the above could be multiplied indefinitely. They would not enable the reader to form either a dramatic appreciation or a functional understanding of the Apaches or their life way. The flow of mutuality, of hospitality, of the giving and taking of satisfactions; the secure movement of childhood into the fullness of the people's heritage; and the magnetism, the far-ramifying suggestiveness of the symbols and the symbol system, all elude the piling up of factual details. But a reader who is willing to read patiently and long, and to turn back more than once in the reading as new significances appear, has waiting for him in Morris Opler's *An Apache Life-Way* an experience not less rewarding than that which the richest novel or biography can yield. Opler, a competent and rigorous anthropologist, traces through from birth to death the life course of an Apache boy and girl, within the social and ceremonial setting of Apache existence. His picture is that of the Mescalero reservation of fifty years ago. The extremely brief account which I have written here, also relates in the main to a time some decades ago.

For the Apaches have been swept into the modern commercial economy. They have moved into that economy as tribal Indians move, and much that was strong and fair in their life has not died, yet deep change has come. Let us see in what fashion the Jicarillas have moved.

As stated earlier in this chapter, the Jicarillas, in New Mexico near the Colorado line, were a fast-dying people until well into the 1920's. They are fast increasing, now.

Their economy had shifted from the chase and war and, subsequently, government rations, to sheep raising. They were serviced by a single trader, known far and wide as a benevolent dictator. From Emmit Wirt the Jicarillas did all their buying, to him they sold anything they sold; he was their banker and credit source and their human counselor.

But Emmit Wirt grew old. His pride and caring were great, and to no one whom he knew could he entrust the business monopoly and the kind of spiritual overlordship which were his own. Wirt was one of the intensely etched personalities of the old American Southwest.

Out of this situation, it came to pass that Emmit Wirt and the Indian Service (I was then Indian Commissioner) laid before the Apache tribal council the suggestion that the Apaches transform themselves into a co-

84

operative commonwealth. Well I remember the long daylight session, out-doors, when slowly through an interpreter I told them about the consumer cooperative movement, its faint and humble beginning in England a hundred years ago, and its spread across the world. Their response was slow; I had no doubt that it would be sure.

The Jicarillas already were an organized and incorporated tribe, under the Indian Reorganization Act of 1934—the act which marked the great change from Indian liquidation to the Indian gathering of power. As a corporation, they were chartered to enter upon tribal business enterprise; as a political body, they were vested with home rule. But as we have seen, the Apaches are a people very near to "primitive" ancient man. It has been the universal presumption of modern Western nations that "primitive," "backward," nonliterate, nonindustrial peoples need generations or centuries for the learning of how to handle themselves within the modern political and economic forms. And specifically, we have noted that prior to their subjugation the Apaches never had organized above the band level, while in the years following their subjugation, into the 1920's, they had lived as mere prisoners, government rationed and repressed.

The Jicarillas met their challenge with quiet, perfect adequacy. From the revolving credit fund established under the Indian Reorganization Act, they borrowed some hundred and fifty thousand dollars. They purchased, on equitable terms, all of Emmit Wirt's business, lands and other assets. They organized a cooperative, through which they purchased all the goods they purchased anywhere, marketed everything they produced, banked all of their moneys, and borrowed what they needed. Their enterprise was a business success from the first day; the government loan was paid off in five years.

The Jicarillas owned their lands individually; that is, the government had "allotted in severalty" their tribal range, with the stated intention of thus implanting a "go-getting" ambition in them, and educating them to political and industrial efficiency. Between the 1880's and the 1920's, allot-ment was forced upon most of the Indians of the United States, and it worked general havoc. Indians of the whole country lost 90,000,000 acres of their best land to whites, through the workings of land allotment, between the years 1887 and 1933.

The Indian Reorganization Act of 1934 authorized Indians who might incorporate as tribes to return their individualized lands to tribal ownership if they wanted to. Every Jicarilla proceeded to return his land. There were no campaigns, no pressure, and no pecuniary consideration. The people are one, the people and the land are one, the land should be one; the Earth Mother should not be "allotted in severalty." Thus the Jicarillas made good on the profoundest, most universal attitude of the tribal Indian throughout North and South America.

A like record, circumstantially varied, could be given of each of the four main Apache groups—the other three being at Mescalero, at White River, and at San Carlos in Arizona. The Mescaleros borrowed $284,000 from the Reorganization Act revolving credit fund, principally to capitalize a cooperative buying and selling organization and to improve their houses and diversify their agriculture; and the loan is now repaid in full. Each of the Apache groups thoroughly organized politically, with home rule under organic acts called Constitutions, which they themselves formulated with advice from the Indian Service. They are among the many Indian tribes which disprove that presumption of modern Western nations and cultures which furnishes the intellectual support of continuing colonialism—the presumption that lifetimes and centuries must pass before "backward" peoples can become fit for liberty. Not in centuries, but in less than ten years, these Apache "primitives" of Stone Age culture have demonstrated a political, economic and technological competence positively superior to that of their white neighbors; they have blazed a future trail for the whites. And they have proved that no incompatibility need exist between the epoch of "primitive" ancient wonder and the values and imperatives which are most modern; nay, that the ancient wonder provides motivation, solidarity, energy and wisdom needed for adequate action in our difficult modern day. This which they have proved is of moment to the whole world. It shows what can be for the nonliterate and nonindustrial peoples who number twelve hundred millions.

Chapter 8

FRANK HAMILTON CUSHING
AND THE ZŪNIS

IN THE year 1879, Frank Hamilton Cushing first entered Zuñi pueblo. He was twenty-two years old. Self-taught, he had been a discoverer in archaeology and anthropology since nine years old. He had created his own museum, on his father's homestead in central New York. At seventeen years, he was publishing scientific reports through the Smithsonian Institution. A physical weakling in his childhood, he had immersed himself in wild nature, and through this immersion had passed on to the life of the Indians. Cushing was an individual of many-sided genius. His observation was precise and insatiable, his analysis and generalization was cautious but profound, and he wrote with such *élan* and beauty as no other American scientist, unless it be William James, has exceeded.

Cushing lived at Zuñi for five years. He mastered the Zuñi language, learned thoroughly the Zuñi arts and industries (for he had manual genius too), and was adopted into the ancient Macaw clan. The sacred name "Medicine-flower," borne by only one person in a lifetime, was given him; he was initiated into tribal fraternities, and gradually was inducted into the religious mysteries and rites, and he became the Head Priest of the Bow, next to the highest priestship in the tribe. In subsequent years, he did basic work in pueblo archaeology.

Into ten years Cushing packed the experience of human centuries. Then his health failed. He was able to write his priceless books, and in Florida he resumed his archaeological explorations. He died in 1900 at forty-three years of age, many years too soon.

Cushing's *Outlines of Zuñi Creation Myths* was published in the 13th Annual Report of the Bureau of American Ethnology, 1891-'92. The volume is out of print, but can be found in most large libraries and all anthropological libraries. Cushing's report is a classic which time and new publications will never make out of date; indeed, new publications do but make its greatness more evident. Cushing is an immortal.

His report cannot be summarized in this chapter. It cannot be summarized at all, because it represents the utmost of concentration, in greatness of words. One who desires to experience a civilization as rich as that of ancient China, and far more strange yet more relevant to our present enigmas, is referred to its pages, and also to *Zuñi Breadstuff,* by Cushing, reprinted in 1920 by the Museum of the American Indian in New York. Only one among the central revelations of Cushing's books is imperfectly summarized here.

Zuñi's organization, Cushing finds, is *mytho-sociologic.* It is an organization very complexly structured, and every structured part of it, and the whole, symbolizes and embodies a view of the nature-world and of man's part in that world.

This nature view and nature union, which the organizational structures symbolize, come down unchanged from times very long ago. Into the Zuñi myths, for example, no element from the white world has entered, though white contact has extended across four hundred years. Wars—countless wars—migrations, pestilences, long famines, have not eroded or changed the multiple complication of social system and mythic symbolism wherein many-sided life, fierce yet gentle, wild yet sweet, is lived out.

Some details must be given, in order to suggest an amazing significance which the Zuñi mytho-sociological organization holds.

When Coronado discovered Zuñi, there were seven towns, "the Seven Cities of Cibola." Today, there is one town, with seven "wards" which are the geographically separated towns of old. Up to Cushing's time there were nineteen clans. Each of these clans belonged to one of the seven divisions (towns, wards), and each of the divisions mytho-symbolically represented one of the seven directions: north, south, east, west, the upper world, the underworld, and the *midmost.* The midmost, thus verbalized as a direction, actually was a center, a synthesis of the other six directions; it pervaded all the others, was their union, their "spirit of the whole."

In order to build up the significance of the above, some paragraphs of Cushing's must be quoted:

By this arrangement of the world [and of Zuñi society] into great quarters, or rather, as the Zuñis conceive it, into several worlds corresponding to the four quarters and the zenith and the nadir, and by this grouping of the towns, or later the wards (so to call them) in the town, according to such mythical division of the world, and finally the

Frank Hamilton Cushing and the Zuñis

grouping of the (clan) totems in turn within the divisions thus made, not only the ceremonial life of the people, but all their governmental arrangements as well, are completely systematized. Something akin to written statutes results from this and similar related arrangements, for each region is given its appropriate color and number, according to its relation to one of the regions I have named or to others of those regions. Thus the north is designated as yellow by the Zuñis, because the light at morning and evening in winter time is yellow, as also is the auroral light. The west is known as the blue world, not only because of the blue or gray twilight at evening, but also because westward from Zuñiland lies the blue Pacific. The south is designated as red, it being the region of summer and of fire, which is red; while for an obvious reason the east is designated white (like the dawn light); while the upper region is many-colored, like the sunlight on the clouds, and the lower region black, like the caves and deep springs of the world. Finally, the midmost, so often mentioned in the following outline, is colored of all these colors, because, being representative of this (which is the central world and of which Zuñi in turn is the very middle or navel), it contains all the other quarters or regions, or is at least divisible into them. . . .

No ceremonial is ever performed and no council ever held in which there is the least doubt as to the position which a member of a given clan shall occupy in it, for according to the season in which the ceremonial is held, or according to the reason for which a council is convened, one or another of the clan groups of one or another of the regions will take precedence for the time; the natural sequence being, however, first the north, second the west, third the south, fourth the east, fifth the upper and sixth the lower; but first, as well as last, the middle (midmost). . . .

Finally, with much to add, I must be content with simply stating that in the high degree of systematization which has been attained by the Zuñis in thus grouping their clans severally and serially about a central or midmost group, we may see the influence of the coming together [very long ago] of two diverse people acting upon each other, favorably to the development of both, in the application of such conceptions to the conduct of tribal affairs. It would seem that the conception of the midmost, or that group within all these groups which seems to be made up of parts of them all, is inherent in such a system of world division and tribal subdivision corresponding thereto. . . .

This notion of the "middle" and its relation to the rest has become the central fact indeed of Zuñi organization. . . . It has given rise to the office of the mortally immortal K'yak'lu, keeper of the rituals of creation, from which so much sanction for these fathers of the people is drawn; to the consequent fixing in a series like a string of the sacred epics, a sort of inchoate Bible; . . . and finally, through all this accumulated influence, it has served to give solidarity to the Zuñi tribe at the time of its subdivision into separate tribes, making the outlying Pueblos they inhabited subsidiary to the central one and, in the native acceptance of the matter, mere parts of it.

Now for the "amazing significance" of the Zuñi mytho-sociological organization, referred to above.

According to season, and according to the subject matter of councils, precedence or leadership shifted from one division to another; but the midmost, made up of all the divisions and reaching through them all, was ever "first and last," holding in reserve a precedence and leadership which no situation or event could gainsay. Zuñi society was (and is) democratic but pluralistic, a society of societies, a nation of nations. Differing responsibilities for different parts, all equally momentous and honored, were (and are) reposed in the sundry divisions; and the multiple pluralism was (and is) holistically made one, and kept one through ages, with no surrender of the pluralistic richness and freedom. *Zuñi, like the Six Nations Iroquois Confederation of old, not merely foreshadows the democratic, pluralistic and holistic world order to come. It possesses and lives by the organizational principles which must be those of the democratic, pluralistic, holistic world order which must take form in the years and centuries to come.* The Six Nations League is gone into the past, but Zuñi and the other Pueblos are with us still.

Had Cushing lived longer, he would have had occasion, I believe, to controvert two errors which have persisted with a curious stubbornness in some of the anthropological literature dealing with the Pueblos.

One of these errors is that the Pueblos have a weak social organization which is likely to break up when vicissitudes befall them. They have no strong central authority, it is said, to impose continuing union on them. Hence, it is said, when the great drought came in 1276, and lasted unbroken for twenty-three years, and no crops could be grown, and the animal life moved to where distant herbiage could be found, and even the springs of drinking water disappeared, the great Pueblos of the thirteenth century broke into fragments. And the breakup, since 1890, of Oraibi, on the Hopi Third Mesa, is cited as being typical. But Oraibi suffered extreme and persevering manhandling by the old Indian Bureau; missionaries rent it asunder; its ceremonial cycle became lost. It was an atypical pueblo, torn apart by an atypical series of white-man actions. As for the great Pueblos of the thirteenth century, had they had a strong central authority forced upon them, which made them stay where they were, they would have perished utterly.

Not strong central authority, but that social genius of pluralistic holism, which Cushing described at Zuñi, has kept the Pueblos undissolved while ages of time, and wars, famines and forced migrations have rolled over them. Forcibly dominating, central authority is contrary to that particular kind of social genius, a genius of freedom within complex and reciprocal structure, which has enabled the Pueblos to outlast all else besides. And their great

Frank Hamilton Cushing and the Zuñis

political-social significance today is their achievement of freedom within order, order within freedom, and pluralistic unity.

The other error is that Pueblo ceremonialism is merely imitative magic and propitiatory gesture, the rote execution of symbolic motions which need not, according to alleged Pueblo belief, have inwardness. Again and again, some anthropological writers have repeated this error. They have not seen or felt the greatness of impassioned art, the joyfulness and the winging onward rush, the solemnity of mood, of those rituals which for their efficacy, according to the express belief of the Pueblos, require of their performers intensity of spiritual passion. The blindness is hard to comprehend. Those who cannot go to the Pueblos will find correction of the blindness in Cushing's books, among other books. But let those who can, attend the Zuñi Shalako ceremony of each mid-December.

There, across the desert at sundown, often across the swirling snow, they will see the gods from the sacred places, hugely masked, and very tall on long stilts, slowly march to bless the new homes of the Zuñis. Hundreds of sheep have been killed for the ceremonial feasting and social feasting, and thousands of Navajos, the Zuñis' enemies of centuries gone, have come as guests, darkly resplendent with turquoise and silver. From house to house, all night, the masked gods go, and many costumed dancers with them, and the mudheads—sacred clowns and potent healers, members of a very ancient priestly society. The sacred clowns are almost naked; they move very slowly in the zero air, with never a shudder of cold.

The Shalako, like any of the great ritual dramas, would require hundreds of pages for an adequate description and interpretation; here it is not described, but is only characterized as being a complex, orchestrated, spacious and exquisite production of art. Every motion, every song, every mask and costume is a mature perfection, every swift rhythm is borne within mightier rhythms of the drama as a whole, and mirth is blended with all the solemnity. I myself have witnessed the Shalako only once, and that was twenty odd years ago: it remains in memory the crown of all experience I have had of the drama, and the image formed around it is that of the singing of all the birds of the world in some miraculous orchestration.

Zuñi pueblo lives by sheep, by farming, by varied and powerful craftwork, and by the bread of the soul; and always, the thought about Zuñi is accompanied by the thought about Frank Cushing, the nature-charmed white man who penetrated more deeply and splendidly, perhaps, than any other into the life of the Indian, and so into one of the hopes of the world.

Chapter 9

IN WORLD PERSPECTIVE

THE Southwestern Indian tribes have a message for the world. The message is of unexceeded urgency, one dares to suggest. It is delivered to a world in terrible need.

How can the message be told in few words?

Mankind is probably a million years old. Language, fire, tools, and human society, according to the slowly enlarging archaeological evidence, probably are a million years old.

Through ninety-nine per cent of that huge time—down to a few hundred years ago in Europe, down to the present in Africa, Indonesia, India—mankind lived the determining part of its life in face-to-face, primary social groups: in village communities and federations of village communities. A wide literature deals with the village community. If one book among hundreds were to be named, Prince Peter Kropotkin's *Mutual Aid* would be that one. In the forty-seven years since *Mutual Aid* was given to the world, science has greatly enriched the data on village communities but has not amended the thesis of Kropotkin.

That thesis was that democracy—political, social, and economic democracy, complexly realized all together—is ancient on earth; that cooperation and reciprocity were the way of men through many thousands of generations; that the conserving and cherishing of earth and its flora and creature life were man's way through these long ages; that the art of education—the art of informing, enriching, tempering, and socializing the personality, and of internalizing the moral imperatives—was practiced triumphantly by village communities in every continent, without ceasing for tens of thousands of years; and that like countless flowers in a long April of our world, human cultures, borne by memory alone, illumined with all rainbow hues the almost unimaginable thousands of little societies wherein immensities of personality development were achieved across aeons and aeons of time.

There came the world changes which have brought us to where we are. The nineteenth century did not guess, other than in the minds of a few

In World Perspective

thinkers like William Morris and W. H. Hudson and Ferdinand Tonnies and Tolstoy, toward what pit of sorrow and fear the changes were trending. The twentieth century does not guess, but knows. The local community, for most Western men, dissolved. The great society and world community, for all men, unattained. Exploitation in place of reciprocity, working as a silent corrosive in the neighborhood, a tempest and flood around the globe. Wastage of cultures and value systems which ages have made, wastage of natural resources stored by the organic life of a billion years, wreckage of the web of life. Power conflicts, ever narrowing in their emotion-charged dogmatisms, lunging toward war. Things and machines, and exploiters through things and machines, the masters of men. Increasingly, a world of social isolates, but no isolate can remain withheld from the power drives making toward the ending catastrophe.

There is no hope, except in the reattainment of community. That reattainment must commence at the local level, reach to the scale of the world, return myriadly from the world to the local level; for it is locally, and there alone, that the fateful years of personality formation and attitude formation are lived out.

Even now—even still—for half the world's people the controlling society is the local community. India's seven hundred thousand village communities are an example; Indonesia's forty thousand; the hundred thousand village communities in Africa south of the Sahara; the *ejidos* and *comunidades*, from Mexico all down the Cordillera to Chile. Nearly everywhere the village community has suffered ruinously, has become socially diminished, through the workings of land expropriation, debt peonage, forced labor-migration, and all the effects of colonial and free-market economy. Yet the village community abides, as the home and the life-sustainer of its billion human souls.

Now the world message of the Southwestern tribes can be told. Here are village communities wherein visibly ply that social will and social genius of the village communities of old. Here is the ancient magic wand of social dream, embraced within industrial practicality and gallant adequacy to meet the challenges of the present. Here the structure and dynamics and inward-ness of the ancient world-wide village community can be precisely known, and here can be known the processes of change which do not diminish, but deepen, the spiritual core.

Yet still, if there were not in many lands a yearning and striving toward salvation through reattainment of the ancient-modern community, the mes-

Indians of the Southwest

sage of the Southwestern tribes would be delivered, perhaps, in vain. But there *is* this yearning and striving in many lands. Go to the Maritime Provinces of Canada, where the Antigonish movement unites and re-enfranchises a hundred thousand families, to see the striving now. Go to Israel, to witness the striving, more exhaustive and experimental and creative than any other on earth, toward re-attainment of community and of reciprocity and of the conserving man-nature relationship. Go to Gandhi's and Nehru's India, whose future greatness is meant to be based on its ancient greatness through revitalized village communities. The message of the Southwestern tribes is not in vain, because they do not march alone or speak alone; a renewed and growing set and strain of humanity is with them.

> World-wide they bloomed, those forests of the soul
>   Which through uncountable years the hope upbore
> Of all our Race of Man, its joy, its dole,
>   And cosmic genius at the social core.
>
> Myriadfold as the forests of all lands,
>   Myriad in structures of the leaf and bough,
> That golden age, mind scarce now understands:
>   Millennial April, gone to Winter now.
>
> Millennial *Winter*? Ah, I think that here
>   And there in our ice age, our iron span,
> There bide lone forests, in a golden air
>   Blown by the Spirit from since that dawn of Man
>
> When wide across our world reached leaf and bloom.
>   It stands, the ancient forest, and can stand
> Even within our world-encroaching doom;
>   Its living roots strike deep in many a land.
>
> Ancient pueblos, deepening while they change;
>   Israel, the Conqueror, newly litten now
> With flame whose guardians down long centuries range;
>   And Gandhi's hope and will, which do not bow
>
> Under a burden huge as Everest,
>   The living Gandhi's affirmation, far
> Heard 'round our world, which few e'er had expressed
>   Since sank the golden age and died the star.

PATTERNS
AND
CEREMONIALS
OF THE INDIANS OF THE
SOUTHWEST

LITHOGRAPHS AND DRAWINGS

Taos.

Relic of the Insurrection of 1845.

98

Taos Kiva, Where the 1845 Revolt was Planned.

Early Winter at Taos—The Red Deer Dance.

Taos Villager: Plains Headdress—an Importation.

Taos Study I.

Taos Study II.

Taos Study III.

Taos Study IV.

Taos Study V.

Taos Study VI.

The "Turtle" Dance *at Taos Pueblo*.

Target Practice, Taos.

San Geronimo's Day at Taos—Climbing the Greased Pole.

Mission, Taos I.

Fiesta San Geronimo at Taos.

Christmas Procession at Taos.

Evening at Taos.

Study for Deer Dance, I.

Study for Turtle Dance

Study for Deer Dance, II.

Study for Deer Dance, III.

Study for Deer Dance, IV.

Taos Scene, I.

A Pueblo Pleasure Dance (Dog Dance), Borrowed from the Plains.

Taos.

Taos.

Taos.

Valley Taos Communal Pasture.

Cold Spell at Taos.

Irrigators.

Taos Family.

Outskirts of Taos.

Evening at Taos.

Taos Indian Reservation.

SECTION 2. "PUEBLOS" OF THE RIO GRAN

Eagle Dancers of Tesuque Pueblo.

Deer Headdress, San Ildefonso.

Chanting for the Corn Dance.

The Corn Dance—*Season of Pueblo Marriage (Santo Domingo)*.

Commemorating Spain at Zia Pueblo.

Buffalo Dance, *A Totemic Ceremony of Santa Clara Pueblo.*

Navajo Squaw.

Harvest Dance at San Juan Pueblo; a Secular Festival.

The Squaw Dance.

A Rio Grande Pueblo Portrait.

Ridicule of the Whites: Secret Dance of the San Felipe Mimics.

Pueblo Saint's Day at Santa Anna: Her Escort of Corn Dancers.

End of Day's Dancing at a Small Pueblo (Santa Anna).

At the Foot of Acoma Mesa.

Acoma.

Departure of Shalakos.

The Gods' Escort.

Annual Visit of Shalakos, Spirits of the Native Mountains.

Sprinkling Pollen at Zuñi for Shalako's Visit to New-Built House.

Mudhead Chanters Welcome the Shalakos.

The Mudheads Clowning for Their Shalako Visitors.

Siatasha and Siaxtaca, Less Spirit Guests—Zuñi Shalakos Dance.

Wrapping the Offerings During Shalako Ceremony, Zuñi.

Returning to Their Mountain Peak—Giant Shalakos Have Blessed New Zuñi Homes.

End of Shalakos Ceremony—the Mudheads Doff Their Masks.

SECTION 4. APACHE, MESCALERO AND JICARILLA

Remnants of the Jicarilla Apaches Gather for Their Yearly Fiesta.

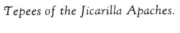

Tepees of the Jicarilla Apaches.

Apaches Butchering a Sheep.

Within the Initiate's Hut—Mescalero Apache Puberty Dance.

Apache Woman.

Apache Supper.

Mescalero Apache Girl Comes of Age—the Dance of the Mountain Spirit.

Mishongovi, Hopi Second Mesa.

Eagle Dancers Are Masked Among the Hopis.

Oribi, Oldest of Hopi Pueblos.

Hopi Snake Dancers I: Antelope Clan Leaving the Kiva.

Hopi Snake Dancers II: The Dance, Possibly the Most Ancient of Pueblo Ceremonies.

Snake Dancer, Hopi.

162

Taos Showmanship: the Borrowed Horse Tail Dance.

Navajo Weaver.

Early Preparations for the Mountain Chant.

The Night Chant—Waiting to Enter Magic Circle of Piñon Branches.

Great Circle of the Feather Dance—Mountain Chant Ceremony.

Levitating the Feathers: Navajo Magicians During Mountain Chant.

Preparing for the Fire Dance.

Climax of the Mountain Chant—*Navajo.*

Rehearsing the Yei-Bei-Chi.

Indian Visitor at the Yei-Bei-Chi.

The Three Gods of Healing and a Medicine Man at Navajo Night Dance.

Last Day of the Healing Ceremony, *The Major Navajo Event.*

Yei-Bei-Chi, the Great Night Chant of Navajos.

The Cow Mask, Navajo Night Chant.

Where Women Take the Lead: Beginning of a Navajo Squaw Dance.

Navajo Portrait.

Oratory at Side Lines of Squaw Dance.

SECTION 6. NAVAJO, PART II

Chee Dodge, the Navajo Statesman.

Squaw.

Squaw.

A Day at the Trading Post.

Navajo Portrait.

Ira Moskowitz

179

Navajo Sketches.

Interior, Navajo Trading Post.

Mother and Child.

Ira Moskowitz

The Secular Side of a Navajo Gathering.

Hogan.

Navajo Camp, I.

Navajo Camp, II.

183

Summer Evening at a Navajo Camp.

Sickness in a Navajo Family; the Hired Medicine Man.

Navajo Shepherd.

Reservation Landscape.

Navajo Country.

Navajo Scene.

Navajo Portrait.

The Cow Mask, Most Sacred of Navajo Yei-Bei-Chi Vestments.

Navajo Camp, IV.

Navajo Camp, V.